Two Plays

PARACELSUS AND PROMETHEUS BOUND

George Ryga

WITH AN INTRODUCTION BY MAVOR MOORE

• TURNSTONE PRESS •

copyright © 1982 George Ryga
"Introduction" copyright © 1982 Mavor Moore

published with the assistance of the Manitoba Arts Council
and the Canada Council

Turnstone Press
201-99 King Street
Winnipeg, Manitoba
Canada

This book was typeset by Triad Graphics Ltd. and printed by Hignell
Printing Ltd. for Turnstone Press.

Design: Darlene Toews

Printed in Canada

Canadian Cataloguing in Publication Data

Ryga, George, 1932-
  Two plays

  ISBN 0-88801-070-2

  1. Paracelsus, 1493-1541 - Drama.
I. Aeschylus, Prometheus bound. II. Title. III. Title: Paracelsus. IV.
Title: Prometheus bound.
PS8585.Y39 3 A19   C812'.54   C82-091358-8
PR9199.3.R9T9

35,835

ACKNOWLEDGEMENTS

Paracelsus first appeared in *Canadian Theatre Review*.

Prometheus Bound first appeared in *Prism International*.

CONTENTS

Introduction 1

Paracelsus 9

Prometheus Bound 107

Introduction

In 1971, with four published plays to his credit, three of them relatively widely performed, George Ryga wrote:

> The resistance to evolving dramatic language and form to meet the requirements of a people and their distinctive national identity still persists. . . . I have had four productions of my work this year in Canada. Every one played to sellout houses and critical acclaim. And yet my position as a Canadian playwright is in a jeopardized situation. There are no breakthroughs yet. Canadian plays are still accepted only as token gesture.

In a later essay on Ryga's work until then[1], I ended with this observation: "An important question for the Canadian theatre is whether Ryga will keep on fighting in the face of so much unrequited success." I need not have worried.

In 1981 he addressed a gathering of popular theatre workers from across Canada and Third World countries in these words:[2]

> I am aware our country is an economic exploiter in areas of the Third World—that as an artist in resistance I have not done enough to catalyse public concern around this issue. The sad fact is that hardly any Canadian artist has focused on this question for a number of reasons. First, so much of our energies have had to be directed to internal problems within the broader umbrella of national independence. We have had to grope through a wasteland trying to find our real history. We have had to break through a colonially-created distrust by our working people of all except closely guarded folk-culture—and to introduce again the contradictions of a class society into our theatre—in a country whose ruling circles deny the divisions and exploitations of classes. We have had to expose racism as part of the economic reality—again, in a country where racism wasn't supposed to exist. We have had to struggle for places to work, for personnel, for research opportunities, for the right to survive, least of all work, in a society that still funds, tours, and artificially maintains an elitist theatre network performing British and American dramatic works in direct opposition to a genuine national theatre—even when this theatre is degenerating into a theatre of the Canadian bourgeoisie. . . .

Behind the political buzz-words (which as always generate more heat than light) can be seen the lineaments of 1980s reality: the march of the new technology and its "global communications." The computer language, says Ryga, "becomes the language of the new colonizers, whose bag and baggage is sophisticated, intricate, complex and seemingly non-violent. . . . Devoid of a sense of self, entire nations become willing consumers for the manufactured pap of one or two mighty industrial giants.'' As a Canadian he understands that process, for ''we are second-class creators of culture in our own homeland, (where) the first one is the recording, publishing and communications industry of the U.S.'' But for his Third World listeners—and despite his express suspicion of ''ruling circles''—he makes what may seem to the unwary a contradictory point:

> Direct meetings across national, economic and political boundaries are critically important. We need the support of our various governments to make such exchanges possible. We also need governmental non-interference to make such exchanges even partially successful.

If Ryga seems at one moment to be a defender of economic and ethnic minorities, at another a champion of regionalism, in the next a raving nationalist and soon after a believer in broad internationalism, the confusion may lie less in *his* conceptual habits than in our own. It is the impulse to create art, not its concrete form, that is universal—though some of its forms may be fleetingly fashionable or perdurably portable across varied cultures. In an age of subcultures and counter-cultures as well as super-cultures, moreover—all fostered by the communications revolution—it becomes increasingly absurd to apply procrustean standards with pretensions to universality. True international exchange is a two-way street, implying something national to exchange; a federal nation (such as Canada) implies regions to federate; a region implies a variety of groups living in one (often characteristic) place; and every social group is composed of individuals, each of whom is also connected to other economic, social and cultural networks that cut across these categories. Pluralistic societies—and the World is one—have much to gain from promoting greater individuality to exchange, and everything to lose from homogenization.

It is an emphasis on the importance of the individual that informs George Ryga's work throughout, and explains better than anything else his continuing course as a playwright. He has always been ''an artist in resistance''—in both senses, I think: a resister skilled in the art of resistance.

George Ryga was born in 1932 on a homestead in northern Alberta, then a depression-ridden pioneer province and not the later resort of the oil-rich ''blue-eyed sheiks'' of Canada. Of immigrant Ukrainian parentage, and self-educated after only seven years in a one-room school-house, he grew up full of songs, stories, folk myths and indignation that soon found an outlet in short stories, a novel and radio and television scripts. It was not until he was thirty-two that he turned to the stage. By that time the elements of his thought, his approach to his art, and even his style were already evident: folklore, both spoken and sung (Ryga writes and has recorded the music to his own lyrics); intense sympathy with the individual caught in an impersonal "system"; a keen ear for a wide variety of speech cadences; a profound respect for nature and instinct with an earthy disrespect for pedantry and artiness; and a free-wheeling dramatic style evolved from the mosaic possibilities of the electronic media in which he learned his trade.

His concern for the underdog and his rage at the blindness of his fellow Canadians to the drama that lay unmined all around them led first to the one-act play *Indian*. The setting is symbolic: "flat, grey, non-country." A no-place environment with overtones of homelessness and rootlessness, in which the protagonist is a transient in his own country. "I never been anybody," says the nameless Indian. Attempting to bring him to heel, the government agent replies: "There are laws in this country. . .nobody escapes the law:" That is the Indian's point: being nobody is the only way to escape the alien rules imposed by a society in which he is given no share.

This theme was more fully developed in *The Ecstasy of Rita Joe* (1967), the play that continues to be Ryga's best known and most widely performed. A gigantic raspberry to a nation then celebrating its centennial, *Rita Joe* leaves the naturalism of *Indian* behind and launches into expressionistic, impressionistic and symbolistic techniques: lifting the past and future into the foreground so the present becomes hallucination, using song, dance, mime and lighting effects to fragment his stage. He begins to use the opening situation of his plays (in the case of *Rita Joe* a trial) as a sort of coat-tree on which to hang remembered incidents and future fantasies, often out of chronological order. We get the whole picture only when the mosaic is complete—the form, as Brian Parker has pointed out, of the folk-ballad.

In *Grass and Wild Strawberries* (1969), Ryga used film screens and the physical involvement of the audience. In *Captives of the Faceless Drummer* (1971), he explored new functions for his chorus: breaking out into supporting roles, citing statistics, acting out the emotions of the principal characters. Always alert to new ways of delivering his message and engaging his audience while he does so, Ryga borrowed not only from Brecht but from his European and American activist contemporaries—all the while aiming squarely at his fellow Canadians. Everything was grist to his mill, but the miller's refrain was the same, whether about native rights, the generation gap or terrorism in Québec: Evil is rampant in the world, and the oppressed must do battle against those who keep it there. There are few solutions or blueprints in Ryga's plays, only tragic alarms synchronized with war cries. *Grass and Wild Strawberries*, for example, ends with the young painter Allan finding only ''a determination for a reckoning with society for making him an outcast.'' In the play, he has already opted out himself.

1971, the year *Captives* was produced, was the very year in which Ryga complained that ''there are no breakthroughs yet,'' and that ''Canadian plays are still accepted only as a token gesture.'' In fact, the 1970s marked an explosion of activity in the Canadian theatre. While the larger theatres may have continued (as they mostly still do) to be financially wary of mounting new plays instead of established successes, the smaller alternate groups multiplied tenfold and many of them produced little *but* new works by Canadian authors, some of which became ''standards.'' This may be the theatre that in Ryga's eyes ''is degenerating into a theatre of the Canadian bourgeoisie,'' but it was nonetheless a genuine breakthrough. The problem was not that the revolution failed to occur, but that it was not the revolution according to the gospel of George Ryga. He had done more than most to launch it, but was not among its principal beneficiaries. The tragic dilemma of the odd-man-out was deepened.

Ryga's response was to reach not for a smaller canvas but a larger one. He went abroad on a grant from the Canada Council and tackled an epic international subject: Paracelsus, the eccentric physician of the Renaissance—with, in his baggage as he traversed Europe, Africa and Asia, the most modern of medical issues: efficiency *or* human kindness. Once again the principal theme is that of one individual pitted against the power of the establishment. Once again Ryga sets up a formal coat-tree: a series of conversations between two modern doctors, a man and a woman, that are interwoven with the Paracelsus scenes until they disappear—the dreamers swallowed by the dream. Once again he uses a variegated chorus to represent the minor roles as well as whole societies and the spirit world. But this time the scale is epic, and the speech ambitiously poetic.

As Peter Hay has pointed out, *Paracelsus* is ''very like those historical plays by British or French or American dramatists, with large casts and expensive costumes, that our major theatres are so fond of importing, lavishing their budgets on . . . it needs a minimum cast of 24 to look good, it requires star actors, it needs lots of money. Though Canadian, it cannot, alas, be easily staged in a warehouse, a converted garage, on a third (or fourth, or ninth) stage, with the usual third and ninth-rate budgets.'' In a word, the play seems suspiciously like a dare. The dare has not been taken up yet, although a production is now contemplated (a decade later) in Montreal, and West German Radio is to broadcast a three-hour version.

Peter Hay calls the play ''unfinished—like all works that have not been staged.'' While this is true in a general sense, I do not find *Paracelsus* unfinished except in the sense that Ryga finds no way to resolve the modern envelope play after Paracelsus, in the play-within-the-play, dies. Smartly observant as they are, the modern analogues offer little that Shaw, Chekhov and Bridie (the latter two themselves both physicians) haven't already given us, even if we were incapable of drawing our own parallels. Once the play-within-the-play takes over, as its magnetism requires, Ryga gives us a muscular and vital drama, black and white in its morality but by no means in its portraiture of one of humanity's outcast benefactors. The double irony, whether intended or not, should not be missed: Paracelsus offers men a giant new medical science that they, led by vested power, reject; Ryga offers his fellow countrymen a giant new play that they, similarly blinkered, will not produce. The irony might well have been less symmetrical if Ryga had succeeded where his hero failed.

During the next few years, George Ryga saw produced and published *Sunrise on Sarah* and *Plowmen of the Glacier,* the latter being frequently performed on radio in various countries. In both 1979 and 1980, it won awards at the Frankfurt Academy of Performing Arts. But although he maintained his status as an important Canadian writer, both at home and abroad, popular success in terms of numerous productions eluded him. It would be going much too far to say he was an outcast, but he was not ''in'' with either the large regional theatres or the *théâtres de poche*.

It was not unnatural, therefore, that his attention turned, for subject-matter, to the greatest outcast in mythology, the Titan Prometheus, famous as a benefactor to mankind—nor that he should see in Prometheus bound echoes of Jesus crucified. Aeschylus' *Prometheus Bound* one of a trilogy) had already found one successor in Shelley's *Prometheus Unbound*, and later dramatists including the

American William Vaughan Moody had written of the great fire-bringer. Once again, however, Ryga wanted to draw a contemporary parallel, so he wrote "a modern adaptation of the drama by Aeschylus."

Altogether aside from the modern setting and (for the most part) language, Ryga's alterations to Aeschylus' seminal play are instructive. To begin with, human history is not predicted but has already happened—it is, after all, already now. Prometheus is enchained not in a rocky gorge under a hot sun and all the elements of nature but in "an abandoned cavern under the earth where some military or isolated technological facility had once functioned." Almighty Zeus has been demoted to First Minister of the country. It is Force and Power who shackle Prometheus to his rock, not the blacksmith Hephaestus—and Force has become a woman! Instead of a chorus, we find only a Farmer and a Worker. The exiled wanderer Io has become a whore, and Oceanus, father of the world's river gods, is reduced in rank to Admiral. But Ryga's modernized version is no *reductio ad absurdum*, rather a carefully worked out and deeply respectful paraphrase.

He cannot, of course, escape the difficulty first faced by Aeschylus: to build a play around a central character who is immobilized. Instead of action we get perforce a series of conversations with visitors—surely more awkward in a cave than out in the open, even if it is symbolically "an enormous tomb for debris and dead things of the world above." But the symbolism is useful for Ryga precisely because he is dealing with the accumulated here and now, not with the mythical past or the projected future. Aeschylus' profound question was: "If the divine power is beneficent, why is there evil in the world? Why do men suffer?"—and Ryga poses the same question to our times. If he fails to answer the question, so did Aeschylus.

In her notes to *Prometheus Unbound*, Mrs. Shelley says that her husband "believed that mankind had only to will that there should be no evil, and there would be none. . . . The subject he loved best to dwell on was the image of One warring with the Evil Principle, oppressed not only by it, but by all—even the good, who were deluded into considering evil a necessary portion of humanity; a victim full of fortitude and hope and spirit of triumph emanating from a reliance on the ultimate omnipotence of Good."

This is also, as we have seen, George Ryga's favourite subject: the individual warring with what he views as the evil in society. Evil in our day he sees as rampant technology, putting unprecedented power into the hands of "the weak/ Who make it their affair/ To learn the mastery of government!" His Prometheus calls for "a new revolution"—but there is terrible irony in the fact that the Prometheus of mythology was the father of technology as well as art.

The theme may be universal, but to Canadians it sounds a particular and present alarm. Almost alone of our playwrights, George Ryga continues to sound that alarm. But if he is successful in arousing his countrymen, he may lose his status as "an artist in resistance." As the painter Allan rhetorically enquires in *Grass and Wild Strawberries*: "What have we gained, when a successful revolution becomes establishment the moment it succeeds?"

But a revolution may be something other than the turfing out of one establishment and the installation of another. The gain may lie in the degree to which we can convince a society and its governments of the importance of the human imagination. If that *conviction* is established, a wise society will use its resources to provide a chance (which is all it can provide) for its own gadflies and dissenters to make their invaluable contribution. In this sense, George Ryga's revolution is getting some place, and he has already rendered great service to both his cause and his society. He will continue to do so best as "an artist in resistance."

Mavor Moore,
October, 1982

[1] Mavor Moore, *Four Canadian Playwrights* (Toronto: Holt, Rinehart and Winston of Canada, 1973), from which portions of the present essay have been gleaned.

[2] *Canadian Theatre Review*, no. 33 (Downsview: York University, Winter, 1982).

Mavor Moore, professor of theatre at York University, was founding chairman of the Guild of Canadian Playwrights and is currently chairman of the Canada Council.

Paracelsus

Dramatis Personae

A cast of 24 players, from which are drawn the secondary characters in the play. Human bodies must be used to texture the play with a sense of humanity relentlessly moving out of one epoch into another. This may be specifically medieval, or it may not.

The four principal players are:

PARACELSUS
FRANZ, his student
DR. PATRICK WEBB, a young medical doctor
DR. BETTY GUZA, his colleague in a contemporary hospital

ACT I

Curtain up.

Three level stage. Lowest front level is sterile and tidy. This setting has a table that contains a coffee urn at one time — lab equipment at another. Two or three chairs.

Second and third levels are progressively darker and more medieval. The more distant and higher the set becomes, the more brooding and aged its atmosphere. There must be tension and violence in the set, but at all times it is only the canvas against which the pageant of human suffering is played out.

SOUND: *Bells of Einsedeln.*

Faint silhouette light over highest level.

Barking of dogs. People fleeing in silhouette in rags, with their possessions over their shoulders. Movement of people is continuous. Soon, some are armed with staves, and turn to fight back imaginary animals and attackers, as others flee past them. This gives way to defenders with swords. Now the injured are being helped as they flee for refuge.

Sounds of gunfire, and crude muskets replace the swords. Men carrying hammers and scythes pass these to fleeing women, and picking up guns, turn to their unseen attackers, fighting as they retreat. Puffs of red light over sound of distant cannon fire.

Action and sound accelerate now. Distant sound of the ''Marseilles'' and fragments of songs from the German peasant rebellions, Russian revolution and the Chinese ''Chilai.'' Rattle of machine guns, roar of aircraft, sound and flash of bombings.

Sudden end to panorama of flight and battle. PARACELSUS *rises from back of set in silhouette, dressed in homespun robe. The people rise around him, bringing their wounded and sick. He heals them. They offer him goods and money. He dismisses the gestures with an abrupt, angry motion.*

An insane woman is brought to him in manacles. He releases her, then holds her head until her wild movements subside. Similar actions of healing and compassion are played out during scene on lower level of set.

Light on lower level of set. Sound of bells abruptly out.

Two interns, DR. BETTY GUZA *and* DR. PATRICK WEBB, *both dressed in medical attire, approach each other from opposite sides of stage.*

DR. WEBB: How is she?

DR. GUZA: She's dead . . . there was nothing we could do for her.

DR. WEBB: I'm sorry. Will you join me for coffee in the canteen?

DR. GUZA: Not just yet.

DR. WEBB *shrugs and turns to leave.*

DR. GUZA: There was nothing more we could do for her, Patrick. . . . You understand what that means?

DR. WEBB *(Nodding):* I was here four days when my first patient died.

DR. GUZA *(Becoming agitated):* That's not what I want to say. . . . We did everything according to procedures, yet. . . .

Loud laughter of PARACELSUS *from darkened levels of stage.* DR. GUZA *is startled.*

DR. GUZA: What was that?

DR. WEBB: Is something wrong?

DR. GUZA: I heard someone laughing.

DR. WEBB: You've been on call too long, honey . . . let me buy you that coffee.

DR. GUZA *(Insistent):* I heard someone laugh!

DR. WEBB: We've both had twelve hours of surgical duty today. I'd be happier if we could leave after six hours, but we're low people on the totem pole at this hospital, so maybe we'd both better get used to the idea of suffering . . . come on. . . .

Another laugh from PARACELSUS. DR. GUZA *listens intently.* DR. WEBB *moves away, but seeing the expression on her face, returns to her.*

DR. WEBB: Why are you staring at me like that?

DR. GUZA: You . . . heard nothing?

DR. WEBB: Are you feeling alright, Betty?

DR. GUZA: Yes . . . yes, I'm fine. . . . *Stares into distance.* I . . . I sometimes wonder what a dying person in the ward thinks of us!

Another laugh from PARACELSUS. *But* DR. GUZA *responds to it with only a slight movement of her head.*

DR. WEBB *(Smiling professionally)*: If you wish, I'll go through my lecture notes from med school and bring you a detailed report on the psychological responses to death in a metropolitan hospital. But not tonight . . . not tonight. . . .

DR. GUZA: I'm sorry . . . it's the first patient I've lost. And the experience is frightening. When I . . . looked into her eyes for the last time . . . I was scared. I wondered what I was doing here . . . or if I was fit to be a doctor.

DR. WEBB: Hey — come on! We're doing the best we can with the finest support systems in the world, Betty.

DR. GUZA: But it's not enough!

DR. WEBB: You and I know it's not enough . . . but to the sick and helpless world out there we're magicians . . . we're like gods in the things we do with the human mind and body!

DR. GUZA: Are we treating illness, or only the symptoms?

DR. WEBB *(Grinning)*: That kind of question is one sure way of flunking med school . . . remember Black Mac and his pep talks? *Mimics a military-like medical instructor in a gruff voice.* Disease is the enemy, an' you're the army at war, an' the first stage of a good army is discipline! I want discipline an' I want order . . . in this school an' in your goddamned heads. Is that understood? An' I don't want any questions when I'm talking! A good army doesn't vote!

DR. GUZA: If you still remember all that crap, then you're as sick as he was!

DR. WEBB: Alright! . . . Who in hell knows the difference, Betty? People go to a doctor like they go to a shoe store — they pay for what they came to buy.

DR. GUZA: I lost a patient this evening!

DR. WEBB: And if you don't smarten up, you'll lose another! *Gently now.* Okay — it isn't what it might be, I know. But if a man comes to me asking for a week of illusion, am I to jeopardize my professional career by offering him ten years of difficult life instead? Besides, I wouldn't know how to do it — that's *my* illness as well as his . . . .

DR. GUZA *(Irritated)*: What in hell kind of attitude is that? A girl who should have lived . . . *had* to live according to my charts and test results . . . died on me this afternoon!

DR. WEBB: What do you want me to do — sorrow for her? For you? The name of this game is efficiency and indifference, honey!

DR. GUZA *stares at him, bewildered.*

DR. GUZA: I'm sorry for jumping you, Patrick. That wasn't very professional of me.

DR. WEBB: You're a woman — you have that right. I'm not tough, either, Betty. So when I get through this, I'm going to specialize. The less I know about the patient as an entire person, the happier I'll be. I'm not a missionary. I'm not even very bright . . . .

DR. GUZA: Am I?

DR. WEBB: You don't have to eat yourself up in general practice, Betty . . . there's not a helluva lot of money in research, but that's where you can still make a name for yourself. I can't belong in that league, but you do . . . .

DR. GUZA: That's a silly thing to say.

DR. WEBB: Then are you prepared to see people die in front of you? Baby, you an' I have enough problems just getting by in this world without that. I need more distance between myself and my work. So do you. Come on — I need a coffee.

Both of them move to leave.

DR. GUZA: I wonder what it would be like . . . to be a real healer?

DR. WEBB: A living hell, I'd imagine . . . .

Light out on their exit.

Light up on centre level of stage. An ancient, disintegrating, dusty casket is being closed by hooded diggers, who pick up their shovels and leave. The casket remains in background.

PARACELSUS, old and pained, stands beside the casket, watching. As the diggers leave, he examines the stains on his smock and clumsily rubs dust from his face and clothing.

PARACELSUS: Once more
    My bones have been disturbed . . .
    Pried from the earth . . .
    Examined in the sun . . . pondered over . . .
    Wise pronouncements made
    Over shape of skull—
    Cause of death . . .
    All the nonsense of the learned
    Whom I had to battle while I lived . . .
    Seven times have my bones been moved
    To please some vanity or curiosity
    Of those I could not bear in life . . .
    Other curses has my death endured—
    The legend of a Doctor Faustus
    Branded on my face;
    There is no price in hell or paradise
    To buy my name and reputation!
    In anguish.
    Leave me alone! Let me rest!
    Let what is left of me endure
    Among the poor I healed in Europe,
    Asia, and primordial swamps of Africa!

Sounds of wind and storm.

A candelight procession of people enter and stop before his casket.

CHANT: Paracelsus — save us! Paracelsus!

A MAN *(Frantic)*:
    Cholera surrounds Salzburg!
    We will die as they die
    Beyond the city . . .
    We have no money!
    They treat the wealthy
    They will not help us
    Who are poor . . .
    Paracelsus— we pray to you

16

Rise from your grave
And save us!

A low murmur as of prayer, from the crowd. PARACELSUS, *unseen by them, looks at them and sadly shakes his head.*

PARACELSUS: Good people . . .
I was dead three hundred years
When you last came to me in this way—
Begging as the helpless begged
Since they first saw light and reason
On this poor and ravaged earth . . . .

CHANT (*Soft and reverent*):
Paracelsus . . .
Paracelsus . . . .

PARACELSUS: Those of you who knew me
Through your great grandfathers—
Peasants by the roadside . . .
Beggars, thieves and merchants . . .
Men paid to war . . .
And after war—wounded,
Maimed, starved . . .
Waving the black stubble,
Lost and nameless on the endless plains
Of death
You knew I would claw and chew
The centuries of earth above my bones
To reach you—to touch you—
For we are all first cousins
To the poor.

WOMAN IN CROWD: Paracelsus! Prince of healers — alchemist!
Our death is only hours away!

PARACELSUS: The dust of centuries around my skull
Could not mute your plea . . .
The very earth moaned and twisted
With the outcry of ten thousand persons
Kneeling at my grave . . .
Like Lazarus,
You resurrected me—
A vapour rising from the soil . . .
The odour of my breath more foul
Than the ravages of cholera . . .

The touch of these hands,
Cut a thousand times by scalpels . . .
Burned by acids and essences of metal
So fierce that even gold would flow like wine
Before their gasp . . . .
Unable now to clasp a vial of medication
Or turn the pages of a book . . .
Still called upon to save a city
Of forgotten, fearful people—
Threatened by an illness
For which I knew and taught
The cure.

WOMAN: Wagoners are falling at the gate,
Twisted with pain! . . .
Rats tear at their still living flesh!

PARACELSUS: Soundless I shriek
From within the earth—
Destroy the rats!
Light fires with cornhusks and oil
In every lane and passage!
Fast your bodies! . . .
Isolate the living from the dead
And dying! . . .
Feed the children only grain
And water from the deepest wells! . . .
And avoid the doctors who examine
First your purse and then your bodies
For they are murderers
Now and always!

WOMAN: We cannot wait! . . . Paracelsus!
Your spirit is alive—save us!

PARACELSUS: God, in your alchemy of blood and spirit—
Help me who has neither now,
To reach them!

Pealing of the bells. The people huddle and move off stage. PARACELSUS *sits wearily beside his casket, his head in his hands.*

Bell sounds die.

DR. WEBB *and* DR. GUZA *enter on lower area of stage and approach the table, which has a coffee urn and cups on it. They pour themselves coffee and sit at the table.*

DR. WEBB: Tired?

DR. GUZA: I'll say. I called my sister to put my son to bed. A year of nights here and he won't know me.

DR. WEBB: How many children have you got?

DR. GUZA: Just the one. Jerry is studying for the ministry, so the next is about five years away . . . .

DR. WEBB: Janis and I couldn't make it. . . . It was a med school marriage . . . .

DR. GUZA (Smiling): She worked while you studied — and then the doctor graduated, looked around and felt he was cut out for bigger things!

DR. WEBB (Irritated): You've no right to make such assumptions! You don't know the story . . . .

She laughs.

Enter a TRADESMAN *and a* MASON *on highest level of set.*

TRADESMAN: With you, it was the same?

MASON (Nods):
> He came to me . . . in a dream!
> He assured me
> That all the minerals and essences
> Of life . . . were now in harmony
> With those of death!
> That I was not to worry for myself
> Or for my children . . .
> That I was to stay home
> And amuse myself and them with laughter
> And with songs . . .
> And not dwell on pain or fear . . .
> For the body excites that which it dreads . . .
> As a fearful man excites an angry dog!

DR. GUZA: If you were to marry again, what sort of woman would you look for?

DR. WEBB: I would want obedience and beauty!

DR. GUZA: As in a house-dog?

DR. WEBB (Grinning): As in a sailboat . . . or a European sports car!

They both laugh.

TRADESMAN: It was the same with me! I drank
    Red wine and tea of ancient herbs
    My mother left within the attic
    Of my house!
    Did you see him in your dreams?

MASON: I recognized him, but no,
    I didn't see him . . .
    His presence was like balm . . .
    And I drifted into deepest sleep.

DR. GUZA: You have the makings of a first-rate bastard!

TRADESMAN: We should show our gratitude
    With candles and with flowers
    At his grave.

MASON: No. Sebastian—let what is, be . . .
    The authorities and church . . .
    Have not forgiven him for what he was . . . .

TRADESMAN: Will they ever?

MASON *and* TRADESMAN *exit.* PARACELSUS *looks up, his face lit with excitement.*

PARACELSUS: The event is not recorded
    In the history of medicine
    That is respectable and well to do . . .
    But I was there!
    Three hundred years after they
    Had laid me well to rest . . .
    Through metamorphosis of spirit, earth and Fire . . .
    I was resurrected for a time . . .
    Emerging through the pores of earth . . .
    Congealing once again like beads of water
    On an icy glass—
    United with my God,
    For whom I gave my talents
    And my life . . .
    But mindless now,
    And without legs that once
    Crossed the scorching plains of Asia . . .
    Without these hands,
    The uncomplaining servants of my skull

Who ached beyond endurance
With the pain of rickets . . .
And giving all, absorbed
The deadly essences of mercury
And lead that early were
To rack each moving portion of my body . . .
Age my face . . .
Thin my hair . . .
Discard my teeth with bursts of blood and pus—
Reduce my body to a twisted, wizened prune
Of age and agony . . .
With claws for hands,
Deformed legs,
Toes curled around each other
Like stubs of dying vines . . .
All this before my fortieth year . . .
Brothers of the sleepless night!
Sisters who have sat with death
Beside the cradle —
My return to you was both the privilege
Of victory and hell!
For I healed quickly,
Free of the encumberance of flesh—
Roving like a flash of light
Through alleys, hovels, the marketplace,
Factories and caverns of the city
Touching with my medic
The fearful and the ill—
Reviving them to face the holocaust of pain
Like seasoned soldiers . . .
For though I found that honest brothers
Of my calling
Had devised new instruments
And perfected knowledge of the human body
Their healing was still blinded
By the ancient ignorance that fails to see
The harmony of God, stars,
Earth and man!
Pain is not the illness,
But a symptom of cosmic discontent
Whose qualities and cure
Are witnessed by a withered leaf . . .
A grain of troubled granite—

The tides and furies of the oceans,
Moon and stars!

Through this speech, DR. WEBB *and* DR. GUZA *are in animated, silent conversation, laughing and jesting with each other.*

Tolling of the bells of the Black Madonna begins.

PARACELSUS *rises to his feet and limps forward, away from the casket. He winces with pain.*

A YOUTH *in turtle-neck sweater, jeans, enters on* PARACELSUS' *level. He carries a notebook and camera. Near the casket he stops and looks around with unseeing eyes.* PARACELSUS *watches him.*

PARACELSUS *(Bitterly)*:
Yet another stranger
Comes to visit me . . .
A poet on the much travelled road to Einsedeln.
The last one made a devil out of me,
Which pleased the charlatans
As apples please the swine!
You poets, scholars, mystics,
I linger as a chill presence
In the windy hollows of your minds.

Sound of bells dies out.

PARACELSUS: Some wise and gentle men along with many fools
Have rummaged on the edges of my works . . .
Translating that which fortifies their arguments—
Quoting passages to prove me nothing
But a raving lunatic . . .
Fortifying a misbegotten faith
That I was prince of wizards,
Capable of darkest, fearful magic
For my ends . . . .

The YOUTH *has opened his books, scribbled a note, and now exits.*

DR. GUZA *has become pensive as she rises to refill her coffee cup.*

DR. GUZA: My grandmother was a Polish peasant woman . . . .

DR. WEBB: Mine was an Empire Loyalist — true red, white and blue she was . . . .

On upper level, enter the hooded figure of a WOMAN, *who moves very slowly, watching* PARACELSUS.

PARACELSUS (*Harshly*):
> She hangs above me still,
> Her eyes inflamed with lust—
> Her stomach and her breasts
> The scented torso of a whore—
> Her hands like silken shawls
> In a southern wind . . .
> Enticing me with sleep and wealth
> And all the soft indulgences
> Of a gifted healer to bishops,
> Kings and all the high-born harlots
> Of three continents!

On PARACELSUS' *level, enter a gentle,* THOUGHTFUL MAN.

PARACELSUS: I possessed and still possess
> The secret of a thousand years of life
> For anyone I cared to damn this way . . .
> Once, when I offered my beloved friend,
> Erasmus of Rotterdam, the choice
> Of longer life and better health,
> He blanched, and then replied . . . .

THOUGHTFUL MAN: Dear Paracelsus, do not offend a friend,
> Who loves you in this way!
> Already I have lived to see the pain
> My words create for other living men—
> Do not let me live so long that I might see
> All I thought noble, brave and righteous
> Becoming poisoned conflicts
> Drenched in blood and hatred . . .
> Let me live my allotted days with no more pain
> Than is my rightful due . . . .

THOUGHTFUL MAN *exits.* PARACELSUS *laughs.*

PARACELSUS: So I blessed the syphilitic, inbred
> Bodies of our kings
> With Erasmus' wisdom
> And no more . . . .

The hooded WOMAN *gestures off-stage in a stylized movement which gives her the significance of being an angel of evil in the life of* PARACELSUS.

Her action slowly brings out a straggling of rustic medieval people who gather as amused observers to some scene about to be played out.

DR. GUZA: My granny was a religious woman, who had a working relationship with her God. Had God lived in the town where I was raised, she would've baked buns for him and mended his socks. To her, He was just like any other Pole on hard times . . . .

DR. WEBB: Mine would've photographed Him, sold copies of the photo, and kept all the profits for herself!

They laugh and huddle together in amusement.

PARACELSUS *turns angrily on his angel, who moves away a slight distance from him. He shrugs with defeat and turns away from her.*

PARACELSUS: I was born of flesh that could be and was tempted . . .
    Let no lies besmirch the truth of who I was!
    From infancy I was prone to laziness, pride;
    The coarse thickness of a peasant mouth and reasoning —
    The dazzlement of costly clothes—
    The arrogance of a mind superior to those about me . . .
    As a youth, I was portly and insolent,
    Eating often for two men . . .
    Inviting brawls with my foul wit—
    Doing battle at ten metres
    With words more calloused
    Than a peasant's fist;
    More cutting than the rapier
    Of a guardsman to the duke . . . .

Enter two peasant THUGS *at a run, responding to the more urgent beckoning of the hooded* WOMAN. *They stop and peer about them, outraged.*

FIRST THUG: Where is he?
    He'll wish tonight his mother had miscarried him
    Upon the dung-heaps of the river Sihl!

PARACELSUS *(Taunting coarsely)*:
    Have you business here?
    You three-legged cocks
    Hatched by scurvied rats of Basel!

Laughter from the people.

SECOND THUG: There he is! I'll thrash him into silence!

PARACELSUS: Wait, you buglers of the barnyard — wait!

The THUGS *pause uncertainly in face of more laughter.*

24

PARACELSUS: How fortunate I happened on you at this time —
There is a well a thousand metres deep before you!
One step more, and both of you would vanish
In the bowels of the earth!

More laughter. The THUGS *kneel and peer before them. Then rise with rage.*

FIRST THUG: He lies! There is no well.
The street is cobbled to the public square!

SECOND THUG: I'll kill him for this!

PARACELSUS: Go home — you are not fit to raise a hand to!
If I must fight
Let it be with men of wisdom
And the icy nerve of marshals
In the fields of war . . .
And not with braying asses
Whose tails drag like whips
Through piss-stenched alleys
Of inconsequential towns.
I am a countryman with long vision!
I cannot even see you
For the squatness of your stature!
With mock anger. Be gone!
Before my rages,
Trapped like tigers in a cage of iron,
Break free and devour you
Like starving hounds devour two frogs!

More laughter. The THUGS *hesitate.* PARACELSUS *moves to them and stops them with a gesture.*

PARACELSUS: Wait, idiots! Can you read?

FIRST THUG *(Blurting)*: No!

PARACELSUS *(To Second Thug)*:
Can you translate
The Latin mumbo-jumbo of the priest
Behind whose ass you crouch at sermons?

SECOND THUG *nods that he cannot.*

PARACELSUS: Pshaw then — be gone!

More laughter. The THUGS *are defeated. The hooded* WOMAN-ANGEL *applauds with slow, measured claps of her hands, at which the crowd exits. She hovers over* PARACELSUS, *her face now exposed and radiant.*

WOMAN-ANGEL: Oh, the swagger of the dandy —
        Sent to study medicine
        With a ready tongue and empty head!
        What pain it gives him then and now
        To comprehend that lifetimes can be spent
        In weeds that grow no taller than this folly!
        How trapped the humble-born can be
        From realizing that the moment of their births
        Were touched by God through His machinery
        Of stars and chemistry of earth and fire!

PARACELSUS (*Anguished*):
        Begone! I was a simple man,
        Born among the pines!

WOMAN-ANGEL: You were never trained to be a healer!
        A healer, like a saint,
        Is born from time to time
        To remind the human race
        It must aspire to God,
        To rise above the murk of slavery and war . . .
        Above the stature of a beast to other beasts —
        Men, or the implements of men!
        The upright man shrinks only to damnation
        In the face of God—
        To no other judgement
        Is he answerable!

PARACELSUS *turns and points an accusing, angry finger at the* WOMAN-ANGEL.

PARACELSUS: That is *my* credo, devil!

WOMAN-ANGEL: Paracelsus—love me!

People, broken in body and spirit, move in opposite directions around him.
PARACELSUS *reaches out to them urgently.*

PARACELSUS: From the moment of awareness
        I never slept again! . . .
        I devoured twenty centuries of medic wisdom
        In a few scant months . . .
        And then discarded it as false
        And unworthy of my skills . . .
        Side by side with men
        Who scarce resembled men

I crawled on my hands and knees
Through damp and dusty mines
Of Germany and England . . .
Examining the lungs and skin of miners,
And searching for the cures
I knew were near at hand . . .
If only I might have openness of mind
To find and rearrange them.
Above the mines, I probed
The earth for gold, zinc, arsenic
And other minerals I needed
For the formulas of ointments, salves,
Purgatives and vapours to blend
With crucible and flame
For the healing needs of patients
Numerous and distant . . .
Ragged, endless as the groping
Soul of man . . . .

He continues attending to the animal-like progression of people around him. He touches and detains a person here and there, gently examining their eyes, mouths, lungs. He vanishes among the people and exits with them.

On lowest level of set, DR. GUZA *and* DR. WEBB *remove surgical masks from their faces.* DR. WEBB *lights a cigarette. Both of them are weary.*

DR. WEBB: That wasn't difficult, was it? From now on our biker's at the mercy of antibiotics and the ability to regenerate bone tissue.

DR. GUZA: He'll be a sick fella in the morning.

DR. WEBB: That's fine . . . it might teach him a lesson in road manners!

DR. GUZA: You sound like a competent policeman.

DR. WEBB: I don't like punks—in hospital or out! I'm sorry if that irritates you, but it's the way I feel.

Three STUDENTS *(two of them the thugs from earlier scene) enter on middle level of set. The* WOMAN-ANGEL *exits as they enter, orchestrating their arrival with movements of her hands.*

The students' clothes are lavish, their manners haughty.

FIRST STUDENT: Who is this fool assigned to teach medicine at Basle?

SECOND STUDENT: More than a fool, I hear . . .
He neither knows Latin

> Nor the civil graces . . .
> Some rustic from Einsedeln
> Who has had quick cures
> For simple ailments, no more.

THIRD STUDENT: A Luther of medicine
> Our more excitable and simple-minded
> Colleagues call him!

SECOND STUDENT: A Luther indeed!
> He will roast upon the spit with Luther,
> And dogs of Germany will lick their chops
> As the tallow of their insolence
> Drips into the street!

FIRST STUDENT: A cunning peasant, though . . .
> Those sent by the church to watch and listen
> Have heard little to condemn him with,
> Save his invitation to the barbers,
> Midwives and other false practitioners
> Of the medic arts
> To attend his lectures.

THIRD STUDENT: Why tolerate this smelly, unwashed scum
> Amongst us—who have paid in gulden
> For our education?

SECOND STUDENT: True — a little knowledge is a dangerous thing
> For the surly beggars of the town!
> How can they comprehend that
> Which they can neither cook nor eat?

Laughter from the three of them.

THIRD STUDENT: It is well he has not loaned them
> Books on surgery
> For they hold their hymnals in church;
> Upside down—and back to front!

More laughter.

SECOND STUDENT: I could not bear today's lecture — I could not!
> Listening to the forest boar grunt and squeal
> About the filth and corruption of our apothecaries —
> I *had* to leave—my sensibilities
> Were outraged by such crudity . . . .

THIRD STUDENT: He is out to maim the Christian practice
　　　　　Of good medicine—but let him squeal.
　　　　　Should his pimple-healing cause one death
　　　　　Then beware Paracelsus, with the pompous name —
　　　　　For we will war with the bandit
　　　　　Who threatens what is our due
　　　　　As doctors!

Like true gentlemen, they somberly shake hands on this commitment. Flickering of flame light over highest levels of set. Distant shouts and cheering.

FIRST STUDENT: How true—for we're not cobblers
　　　　　Or sweepers of the streets;
　　　　　Our profession is a noble one,
　　　　　Built on the sacred rock of Avicenna's teachings.
　　　　　And for this, we shall be paid with lodgings,
　　　　　Clothes and stature beyond the view
　　　　　Of cobblers or draymen!

SECOND STUDENT: Brothers, we worry needlessly—
　　　　　Small rains will fall,
　　　　　Leaving puddles in the street
　　　　　Which the sun of the everlasting Faith
　　　　　Dries in an hour and is forgotten!

Flame lights rise higher. Shouting and cheering increases and comes nearer.

THIRD STUDENT: But should our faith overlook this nuisance
　　　　　We must petition our protest
　　　　　To the university!

SECOND STUDENT: Aye—one must defend oneself
　　　　　Against the squat and ugly toad!

Putting their arms around each others' shoulders, they turn to leave jubilantly.

But a small crowd of other STUDENTS, *poorer and more determined, enter with* FRANZ *at the lead. They are drinking and unruly. At the sight of the three wealthy* STUDENTS, *they stop, embarrassed.*

The three wealthy STUDENTS *realize their momentary advantage, and to goad the poor* STUDENTS, *they fan the air before their faces, as if trying to drive away a bad odour.*

SECOND STUDENT: Ah, but what have we here—
　　　　　A procession of goatherds
　　　　　On their way to dinner?

The poor STUDENTS' *abashment begins to turn to anger.*

FRANZ: Delinquents from the class
Who conspire how to purchase jewellery,
Whores, and positions of influence in medicine!
How dare you be absent
When the great Paracelsus teaches?

FIRST STUDENT *(Flicking his shawl at Franz)*:
Begone . . . begone . . . .
The smell of your unwashed arse offends me!

FRANZ: I'll have my arse upon your face if you
Play the whore with me!

FIRST STUDENT *(Mimicking Franz)*:
I'll have my arse
upon your face . . . .

But he is cut off in mid-sentence with a fist-blow to the shoulder from FRANZ.
The rich STUDENT *is shocked, but immediately responds by a courtly, for-
mal stance for fisticuffs.* FRANZ *laughs, and removing his hat, pelts the rich*
STUDENT *from side to side across the head with the coarse hat.*

FIRST STUDENT: Let's have none of that!
Fight like a gentleman, you swine!

Laughter from the poor STUDENTS, *who form a circle containing the two
combatants.*

FRANZ: Take that! . . . And that! . . . And that!
Ah, your eyes smart — yet there is no bruise
Upon your cheek!
Now you know — that not all wounds are visible!

FIRST STUDENT: You are a coarse villain,
Unfit for the study
Of Avicenna's teachings!

FRANZ *seizes the* FIRST STUDENT, *turns him around and leaps on his back,
riding him gleefully.*

FRANZ: Gallop now, my wealthy gelding!
For Avicenna is no more!
This day, Paracelsus had the books
Of Avicenna burned in the college square!

Dismounts from back of the FIRST STUDENT, *who stares with disbelief at*
FRANZ.

FRANZ: When Paracelsus spoke above the flames,
        The blood began to boil—
        And a great burden lifted
        From our temples and our eyes—
        The very vines upon the walls
        Detached themselves and waved huzzanahs
        To the liberation which we felt!

SECOND STUDENT: They lie! These filthy vermin lie!

Laughing, the surrounding STUDENTS *pummel the three wealthy* STUDENTS *with their hats, notebooks and mittens. The three wealthy* STUDENTS *flee and exit.*

FRANZ: Ah, what a day we've seen, brothers!
        Today was the morning of a great new age in medicine,
        And as true apostles we were blessed
        With living through it!

PARACELSUS *enters on topmost level of set, performing his lecture over* FRANZ'S *lines.*

He is confident, cheerful, the teacher.

PARACELSUS: As town physician and teacher
        At this university—I welcome you,
        Students of medicine . . .
        Students of the art of healing . . .
        Those of you blessed with intelligence
        But cursed with poverty, I take into my house,
        Where, so long as I am able,
        I will shelter, feed and clothe you
        While you learn . . .
        I have led you all outside the city
        Through the hills and fields,
        Seeking herbs where God had placed them—
        For there medicines do grow by choice,
        Drawing from the soil, air and the forge of heaven
        The potent virtues in the great apothecaries
        Of the mountains, valleys, meadows and the forests . . .
        Everything I teach you
        In the simple German language
        Of my birth and yours . . .
        Everything I teach you
        I have learned from experience
        And observation . . .

For nothing must be left to chance
And one published error may cost
Ten thousand lives of patients
In our care . . .
It is a lofty and a serious thing we do —
Healing is a gift of God to Man . . .
There is no oracle we dare not question!

POOR STUDENTS *(Chanting)*:
Down with charlatans in medicine!
Down with rogues and murderers!

PARACELSUS holds aloft two huge books.

PARACELSUS: You have built a flame within the square
Against the chilling northern wind.
I would assist the progress of the fire
By disposing from this ancient school
The spirit of the antique cadavers of medicine —
Avicenna and Galen — who bedevil all enquiry
And have made of healing a priesthood
Of wealth, arrogance and power
Built on teachings which do not bear
The simplest tests of reason or effectiveness!

He hurls the books down.

PARACELSUS: Into St. John's fire now
So all misfortunes of the past
May at last vanish into air with smoke!

A cheer from the STUDENTS. PARACELSUS laughs with them, then grows stern and silences them with a gesture.

PARACELSUS: Let God ordain, and you apply yourselves
In such a manner that our effort to advance
Once more the art of healing may succeed!
One other matter
In which I require your awareness
And sympathetic understanding;
I have this day, as town physician,
Examined apothecary stocks within the city
And found them stale and worthless—
Priced to bring good wealth
To the charlatans who sell them . . .
I have also found

>When I pressed these vandals to the wall
>That they share a secret understanding
>With the doctors—
>To split the profits of their carelessness
>And murderous neglect!

On lowest level of set, a patient enters and is examined by DR. WEBB, *while* DR. GUZA *watches and assists.*

FRANZ: Tell us who these people are, Paracelsus—
>And we shall deal with them in ways
>They understand—
>Or put their filthy practice to the torch!

Three wealthy STUDENTS *return, but remain in background, listening and taking notes.*

A cheer from the poor STUDENTS *greets the suggestion from* FRANZ. PARACELSUS *shakes his head and smiles.*

PARACELSUS: Nay . . . nay . . . there are other ways
>To deal with villainy.
>I have written to the city magistrates,
>*Winks mischievously*
>Who dispense all law!

A wave of laughter.

PARACELSUS: As well as make appointments to the university!

Another, longer wave of laughter.

PARACELSUS *(Sardonically)*:
>I have written to the city magistrates of Basle . . .
>Those grave . . .
>Pious . . .
>Strong . . .
>Foreseeing . . .
>Wise . . .
>Gracious . . .
>Favourable gentlemen!

More laughter on each adjective about the magistrates.

PARACELSUS: I have written to request . . .
>In my capacity as town physician . . .
>That proceedings of apothecaries
>Be rigorously controlled;

Their recipes submitted to me
For opinion of worth—
That appointments of apothecaries
Be examined for approval—
That all medicines be priced
According to their worth . . .
The same rates prevailing
In each apothecary in the city;
That profiteering in the tools of healing
Be forever banished from the commerce
And affairs of Basle!
On this I take my stand
As healer, teacher, chemist—
And let those who profit from corruption
Rage until the pit of hell consumes their furies
And their worthless souls!

A sober murmur of approval. One of the three wealthy STUDENTS *raises a fist to* PARACELSUS.

WEALTHY STUDENT: Yours will be the first soul to roast!
Make no error of the heresy you've committed
Here this day!

FRANZ: Put down your fist, you ninny,
Who stands before this man
But for the graces of your fathers' purse!

WEALTHY STUDENT: The fool who screams revolt
In shelter of forgiving night
Will have a different morning to endure!
All the world's physicians are not wrong!

The STUDENTS *become turbulent, surrounding the three wealthy* STUDENTS. PARACELSUS *comes down among them.*

PARACELSUS: Hold your noises!
Remember why we stand before each other
As students and their teacher!
You are here to learn
That nothing which benefits the sick
Should be denied—
Not your services,
Nor medication,
Nor wisdom—
Nor the charity of pity!

The squeak of fear you heard
Has an element of truth;
A true healer fights for those he serves.
He must likewise be prepared
For the consequences of his mind and deeds —
In this way does God make great healers
On the anvil of his howling forge!
Let us leave now friends —
We have work to do.

The STUDENTS *disperse, except for* FRANZ, *who remains, donning a leather apron, as does* PARACELSUS. *Patients enter and are treated with examinations, salves, lances and oral medication, with* FRANZ *assisting the doctor.*

This action continues over dialogue.

FRANZ: You have turned both my flesh and brain
          Upon that sacred anvil,
          And struck sparks of comprehension
          Like golden arrows through a mired beast . . . .

PARACELSUS: There is no one from whom greater love is sought
          Than from a doctor—beware you understand
          The meaning of this, Franz . . .
          Or flee now from my presence
          As a doe flees the huntsman's spear!

FRANZ: No—let me stay beside you . . .
          I come from Meissen, and have wasted all my money
          In the schools of Heidelberg . . .
          I will demonstrate your lectures . . .
          Run errands in the market for your house and surgery;
          Keep your clothes and notes in order . . . .

PARACELSUS: Poor studious Franz . . .
          There is no fatigue within these bones
          Or skull of mine—
          You will be roused in the deadest
          Hours of night
          When my brain fevers
          Like a newborn star;
          You will enscribe notes
          I dictate to you . . .
          You will suffer
          So that others might be free
          Of suffering . . .

I will make a distinguished doctor
Out of you,
But it will not be
A key to riches and success;
It will be a scar of pain and wisdom
Etched upon your gentle, trusting face.
Your answer at this age
Will be immediate and sure,
But the burden of your life
Rests like a boulder on my neck—
For what if I should fail?

FRANZ: Never! I shall work and study
      With what life is in me!

PARACELSUS: But if I should madden?
      Or bring you to the scaffold
      For your trust in me?

FRANZ *averts his eyes from the withering gaze of* PARACELSUS. *They continue their work with their patients.*

DR. WEBB *and* DR. GUZA *complete their medical examination of their patient. As patient exits, she tidies up.*

DR. GUZA: You have good hands for surgery, Patrick.

DR. WEBB *(Mocking)*: If I can ever be of service . . . .

DR. GUZA: I could never work as quickly or cleanly.

DR. WEBB: Most surgery is routine—if the diagnosis is accurate, the treatment is nothing. I sometimes feel it's as predictable as mailing a parcel.

DR. GUZA: Then why did I lose a patient?

He shrugs and turns away from her.

On uppermost level of stage, PARACELSUS *and* FRANZ *continue their work with patients.*

Enter three wealthy, bejewelled, sophisticated DOCTORS *on middle level of set.*

FIRST DOCTOR: Paracelsus? . . . Does this imply
      greater than Celsus?

SECOND DOCTOR: He certainly has pretensions to Celsus,
      Physician to the emperor Augustus!

FIRST DOCTOR: What pomposity is this
    For an unknown peasant on whom
    The degree of Doctor was never given
    By a university of reputation?

SECOND DOCTOR: Bare-assed-celsus is more in keeping
    For the braggart!

THIRD DOCTOR: His ass is well protected, never fear!
    Despite his lamentations
    The hypocrite lives well.
    The clothes he wears—
    The swagger of his walk—
    All reveal strong pretensions
    To the title ''doctor!''

FIRST DOCTOR: Who of us confronts him in his surgery?
    I do not choose to sully my good reputation
    In challenges with quacks and thieves!

THIRD DOCTOR *(To second Doctor)*:
    There is no danger—you insult him,
    For you alone have read the insolence
    Of what he writes on healing!

Brandishes his cane.

THIRD DOCTOR: Go to it—we'll protect you!
    And if he tends to violence
    We'll have him arrested
    And trundled out of town!

The three DOCTORS *move to upper level of set and approach* FRANZ *and* PARACELSUS.

The SECOND DOCTOR *throws back his shoulders and clears his throat.*

SECOND DOCTOR: Are you called Paracelsus?

PARACELSUS: I am. What need have you of me?

SECOND DOCTOR: We are doctors of this city—tell us,
    Has any physician of repute
    Addressed you as ''doctor''
    To your face?

PARACELSUS: I have met no worthy doctors in this city,
    So the question does not merit a reply!

SECOND DOCTOR *(To his companions)*:
      He has not met a worthy
      Doctor in this city . . . methinks that would be
      As near as he would come to the healing arts!
      To Paracelsus. Do my colleagues then
      Not meet with your approval?

PARACELSUS: Good manners and the dignity of healer-teacher
      Compel me to reply with silence!

THIRD DOCTOR: Ah, ah—be careful now!
      These are learned men you speak to . . .
      Where is your learning from, we ask?
      Or are you a self-appointed peddlar of rubbish
      Whose concoctions of forest droppings
      Might neither help nor hinder
      The passing of some minor ailments
      Had they been administered by the village idiot?

PARACELSUS: My teachers were the finest in the world —
      Ancient and modern masters of their skills . . . .

SECOND DOCTOR: Who were they, then?
      Nowhere in your writings do you . . . .

PARACELSUS *(Impassioned now)*:
      My father was the first . . .
      From him came the title Paracelsus;
      At ten years of age
      I performed surgery at his side . . .
      Surgeon and physician to the town of Einsedeln —
      I dressed wounds . . .
      Helped him blend the salves and potions
      He dispensed. Later in my life
      I entered many universities—
      Gleaning what I could from this learned
      Scholar and from that . . .
      Discarding all which defied experience or reason—
      Many of the masters in whose steps you follow
      I forsook as useless baggage for a healer
      Ere I was twenty years of age!

FIRST DOCTOR: Then you are not a graduate doctor
      From any school of medicine?

PARACELSUS: Test me on my practices
      And not on superficial dressings
      For a healer's pride!

FIRST DOCTOR: You are not a doctor, then!

PARACELSUS *tosses a bloodied bandage in direction of the* FIRST DOCTOR, *who strikes defensively at it with his cane, missing it.* PARACELSUS *laughs and turns to help* FRANZ *blending chemicals.*

SECOND DOCTOR: How many people have you killed?

PARACELSUS: How many have you cured,
      You perfumed dandies
      Overstuffed with capons
      And the wines of France?

SECOND DOCTOR: I ask again—how many patients have you killed
      In your departures from the proven remedies?

PARACELSUS: Thousands have I treated in the mines of Germany,
      France and England against diseases of the lungs
      And heart . . .
      In every city of this continent,
      Into Africa, and east, through the massive
      Lands of Russia—
      Through the Tartar lands and beyond Samarakand
      Where I was held a prisoner of war a time —
      I healed diseases of the skin, digestion . . .
      Gout . . . the injuries of men and women
      At their work . . .
      The ailments of children . . .
      The ravages of madness in its many forms . . . .

FRANZ *(Afraid for Paracelsus)*:
      No! . . . Tell them no more!

PARACELSUS: The imbalances of acid on the body . . .
      Diseases caused by food . . .
      The peculiarities and treatment
      Of the wounds of war . . .
      The affects of poisons
      In the rocks and foliage . . .
      Diseases of promiscuity. . . .

A stream of human bodies passes by, bent, hurt, beseeching help.

FRANZ: These are small men, Paracelsus —
        Let them not draw you into danger!

PARACELSUS: There is no danger, Franz—these vultures
        Know me well, as I know them!

Points to THIRD DOCTOR.

PARACELSUS: This one treated Markgrave Philip of Baden
        To the edge of death when I was summonsed —
        He knows me!
        When I cured that wealthy wretch
        This . . . doctor . . .
        Interfered with payment of my fee.

THIRD DOCTOR: It was higher than the fee
        I asked for treatment of the Markgrave!

PARACELSUS: The many thousand poor I heal
        Without a fee—
        For it is my credo
        And the will of God in Heaven
        That no human be denied relief
        From pain and suffering
        Because he lacks the wherewithal
        To pay a healer.
        Is it not just
        The rich pay for the poor,
        When they starve and bind
        Entire kingdoms to such poverty?

THIRD DOCTOR *(Enraged)*:
        Oh, how fortunate I spoke
        To the nobleman Markgrave
        And persuaded him not to pay a gulden
        To the devil for his guile
        And false medicines!

PARACELSUS *speaks to* FRANZ *now.*

PARACELSUS: When he awoke, when human gratitude
        At absence of all pain still blessed
        That chiselled face of wealthy breeding,
        Markgrave Philip gave me this!

PARACELSUS *holds up a jewel which he wears around his neck.*

PARACELSUS: A useless piece of decorative stone . . .
   I cursed it and have worn it since
   As a burden of humility around my throat
   Lest I forget the baser parts of man!

Turns on the three DOCTORS.

PARACELSUS: Not one person yet has perished in my care,
   Though I have been physician to more people
   Than would populate a nation in these realms
   There are great healers on this earth—
   I know them all, and count them
   On the fingers of this hand . . .
   But there is one Paracelsus only,
   And he has better work to do
   Than fence with chimney-sweeps
   In the temple of the healing arts!

He turns his back on the DOCTORS, *who pull up the collars of their cloaks in the manner of assassins and crouch to rush him with their canes.*

The WOMAN-ANGEL *appears, her hand in terror to her mouth.* FRANZ *is afraid, and grasping a bottle of clear liquid, uncorks it. He faces the three* DOCTORS, *as* PARACELSUS *watches a mad* WOMAN *being led to him, weeping.*

FRANZ: I hold acid here more deadly than the hottest flame —
   I will not hesitate to throw it at you
   In defence of my teacher from attack!

The three DOCTORS *turn away and exit, hooding their heads totally as they leave.*

THE WOMAN *is brought to* PARACELSUS *by a* MAN, *her husband.*

MAN: My wife is mad, Paracelsus, help her!
   All day long she sits before the house
   And weeps.

PARACELSUS *(Comforting her)*:
   Why do you weep, woman?
   The world was sad enough
   Before we came —
   So we must cheer it in the time
   We live!

WOMAN: It is the soldiers passing on the road
   To war—such lovely men . . .

I had a son their age . . .
It is . . . as if men . . .
Were born to die —
I can't endure it, doctor!

PARACELSUS: Have you a cow?

WOMAN: Yes.

PARACELSUS: Does she milk well?

WOMAN: A bucketful at sunrise
And as much at night . . . .

PARACELSUS: And have you extra bread
Now that your children all have grown
And gone?

WOMAN: Yes . . . he and I eat little . . .
We feed ourselves and half the village dogs . . . .

PARACELSUS: Rise early in the morning, then . . .
Milk your cow and bake your bread . . .
Make butter . . .
And when the men who march to war go by,
Invite them in for food,
For they are all your sons . . . .

The WOMAN *wipes the tears from her eyes and stares at* PARACELSUS *a long moment.*

DR. WEBB *sits at a table reading a magazine.* DR. GUZA *enters with a tray of sandwiches. She offers him one.*

DR. WEBB: If medical care was introduced by the government for the first time, would you support it, Betty?

DR. GUZA: Yes . . . the same way I'd support old age pensions.

DR. WEBB: I sure as hell wouldn't!

DR. GUZA: Why not? At least you're sure of payment for your services.

DR. WEBB: I resent losing any more control over my affairs!

DR. GUZA: But medicine is not a personal affair—no more than aging or education is!

DR. WEBB: It bothers you that I can think the way I do, and still be a good surgeon, doesn't it?

DR. GUZA: Yes . . . yes, it does . . . .

WOMAN *staring at* PARACELSUS *smiles.*

WOMAN: The men who march are always hungry?

PARACELSUS *nods.*

PARACELSUS: Gods and murderers alike have stomachs
        Needing food . . .
        Let the helpless sorrow—
        Good women such as you
        Have work to do!

WOMAN: Then . . . I am not insane!

PARACELSUS *laughs and draws her to him with his arm.*

PARACELSUS: Help feed the world
        And you will have
        No further need of me!

The WOMAN *and her husband leave. The three hooded* THUGS *enter, staves in hands. They stand and peer at* PARACELSUS, *who tends to other patients needing reassurance and medication.*

Enter hooded WOMAN-ANGEL, *who moves between the* THUGS *and* PARACELSUS. *The* THUGS *retreat at sight of her and exit.*

PARACELSUS: Are you condemned to follow me
        Through all eternity?

WOMAN-ANGEL: How long will you deny me?

PARACELSUS: Until the earth disintegrates
        And takes its place again
        As dust within the cosmos!

WOMAN-ANGEL: They will crucify you
        As they crucified the bloodless master
        Whom you chose in passion
        To dedicate your thoughts and actions to!

PARACELSUS: It was a choice from which I do not flinch —
        I have endless things to do . . . .

WOMAN-ANGEL: With hands that centuries ago corrupted
        Into soil to feed the roots of graveyard cyprus trees?
        And will you spend eternity exchanging curses

> With decaying scum
> Of medieval Europe?

PARACELSUS: Nothing is in vain—
> My life and work will be remembered!

WOMAN-ANGEL: By whom, Paracelsus? My dear child, by whom?
> A few romantics — who will rejuvenate your memory
> From time to time for some murky truth
> Which irritates them in your work and life
> As blisters irritate a distant traveller?

PARACELSUS: My time is short—begone!

He lights a chemist's distillery which FRANZ *has prepared for him. Bending over his work,* PARACELSUS *trembles.* FRANZ *now takes over care of patients who pass in procession.*

WOMAN-ANGEL: Already, cultists are intrigued
> By the magician in your deeds—
> The darker fears of man
> Make my presence equal to your God, Paracelsus!

PARACELSUS: A lie!
> My courtship with the darker arts of alchemy
> And commerce with the dead was of short duration!
> I sought truth—all that relieves suffering
> Is sacred!

WOMAN-ANGEL: Why lock the deeper secrets
> In your tortured mind?

PARACELSUS: Only the best of what I do matters!

WOMAN-ANGEL: You are dead, Paracelsus—
> Your voice is silent now within the tomb . . . .

PARACELSUS: The chore of turning magic into alchemy
> And then to science shall live
> Beyond me!

WOMAN-ANGEL: Yes—it lives . . . and delights me!

PARACELSUS *looks up at her with anguish.*

PARACELSUS: Why . . . does it delight you, devil?

WOMAN-ANGEL: Did you dream your works would change
> The nature of man's lust for power

Over human life, over mountains,
Oceans and the stars?
No great nobility emerged because
You freed mankind of pain —
And for this revelation,
I do thank you!

PARACELSUS *picks up a clod of earth and throws it at the* WOMAN-ANGEL, *but it falls short. She laughs scornfully.*

WOMAN-ANGEL: I would make a bargain with you—
Not for your soul—that means nothing
While I hold the souls of generals
And heads of states, so powerful
That the very mountains quake before them;
I hold the souls of healers in my hand
Whose avarice would make you blanch with fear
At the history of medicine beyond your day —
They make fortunes and great reputations
Over men in prison
On whose bodies and helpless minds
They conduct the most bizarre and dreadful surgery —
They create disease for which there is no cure;
They create medicines for which there is no illness!

PARACELSUS *cringes. Turns to* FRANZ, *who is oblivious of the conversation.*
PARACELSUS *then faces the* WOMAN-ANGEL, *his face tortured.*

PARACELSUS *(Shouting)*:
You lie! . . . You lie!
Or if what you say is true,
Then some catastrophic changes overcame
The earth. . . .
'Tis true . . . a disorder in the cosmos
Can affect death and madness on the earth . . .
My observations of the great comet
Bore this out . . . .

WOMAN-ANGEL *laughs at him. He becomes confused and searches the darkness and the faces around him.*

WOMAN-ANGEL: For helping me to see
The full depth of human decadence
I could help you to return
To rectify the damage to your name!

PARACELSUS: I made no bargains with corruption in my life,
        Nor will I sacrifice the peacefulness of death
        By entertaining darker spirits in my grave!
        Go away! . . . Go away! . . .
        My great sword—hollowed through the clasp
        And well into the blade as a dry compartment
        For my most valued drugs . . .
        Is lost somewhere in the dust and waters
        Of this world . . .
        My books, crucibles, most elementary tools
        Of alchemy and surgery . . . have mouldered back
        Into the elements of which I made them . . .
        Nothing remains . . .
        Except the spare reminders of my life and time;
        Fashioned out of paper,
        Stone and bronze, by loving hands . . .
        Yet this restlessness beyond the grave persists—
        I have work to do! . . .
        God did not accept me to His bosom
        As I thought He would . . .
        I have work to do! . . .
        There has been neither peace nor wisdom for me
        In my passing through the veil of wind and stars
        Into the icy silence of eternity . . . .

WOMAN-ANGEL *laughs again and exits.*

A TRIBUNAL *of city fathers enters. The three men seat themselves in a formal line in silhouette on uppermost level of set.*

The movement of patients visiting FRANZ *and* PARACELSUS *ends.* PARACELSUS *puts a soiled robe over his shoulders and moves slowly towards the tribunal.*

On the lowest level of the set, DR. WEBB *and* DR. GUZA *are playing chess. She makes a move and leans back in her chair.*

DR. GUZA: Checkmate!

DR. WEBB *(Irritably)*: I find it difficult to play with a woman.

DR. GUZA: That's your tough luck, baby . . . what other hangups have you got?

He peers stonily at her for a brief moment. She smiles.

DR. GUZA: Suppose I wasn't a doctor . . . I was a woman you'd never met, and I came to you asking for an abortion because I had no husband, and it would be difficult for me to . . . .

DR. WEBB: That's enough, Betty! *Glances at his watch.* It's time for my rounds. . . .

DR. GUZA: I'm serious, Patrick.

DR. WEBB: I know you are . . . an' my reply is, I'm in the business of saving life, not destroying it!

He rises abruptly to his feet and leaves. She stares after him thoughtfully.

PARACELSUS *comes to a stop slightly below and in front of the tribunal. The* HEAD OF TRIBUNAL *reads a paper before him.*

HEAD OF TRIBUNAL: These charges are serious, indeed . . .
    The doctors of Basle speak with one voice,
    Condemning your outrage at the university
    And demands you make on healers and apothecaries.
    We have much to ponder here . . . .

PARACELSUS: The outcries are from those who do not *know!*
    A good doctor knows the sick and all pertaining to them
    As a worthy carpenter must know his wood!

SECOND MEMBER OF TRIBUNAL: He is headstrong and proud,
    With pretensions to knowing skills
    Of his profession
    Better than all others. . . .

HEAD OF TRIBUNAL: He does . . . he does . . .
    The record of his cures is known far and wide,
    Although it would be pertinent for him
    Not to advertise his great success . . .
    All of us must not forget
    It was the history of his healing
    Which moved us to invite him to our city
    In the capacity he now enjoys.

THIRD MEMBER OF TRIBUNAL: But his arrogance is now a matter for this office.

HEAD OF TRIBUNAL: True.

THIRD MEMBER OF TRIBUNAL: We risk the loss and hostility of city
    doctors—

Even though Paracelsus is a legend in his arts . . .
The truth is this — we cannot lose the service
Of our men of medicine, be they good or bad!

PARACELSUS: The battle is not of my choosing!
They must conquer in their natures
All which darkens them
And betrays the causes they must serve!

HEAD OF TRIBUNAL *opens another letter and reads.*

HEAD OF TRIBUNAL: This, Paracelsus has addressed to us
In flattering and gentlemanly terms . . . .

THIRD MEMBER OF TRIBUNAL: It's so unlike him.
Perchance the man is ill himself!

Laughter from the three of them.

HEAD OF TRIBUNAL: Nay, he is not ill. *Reads.*
He requests authority to cleanse
The apothecaries of the city
And reduce the profits which they earn.
In truth, the claim has merit,
For we all have seen dispensaries about
Unfit in their condition to be hovels
For the swine!

SECOND MEMBER OF TRIBUNAL: That is not the issue in dispute . . .
A filthy keeper of a shop, like a filthy beggar,
Invites contempt equal to his station . . .
Yet Paracelsus seeks authority to interfere
With earnings of natural commerce
And God-given trust between healers,
Apothecaries and the ill and stricken!
Let a headstrong rebel legislate
The qualities of healing and the healed . . .
And we will then be asked to legislate
Friendship between people in the streets!

HEAD OF TRIBUNAL: What is our decision then?

PARACELSUS: Let your philosophies concern themselves
Only with the problems which I pose!

SECOND MEMBER OF TRIBUNAL: Though he be a pioneer as doctor,
Beholding all things in a newer and truer light,

I am not made of his spirit . . .
And therefore vote against him . . . .

HEAD OF TRIBUNAL *turns to* THIRD MEMBER OF TRIBUNAL. PARACELSUS
paces nervously, huddling within his garments.

THIRD MEMBER OF TRIBUNAL: What I say is not influenced by fear—
I dislike the man, but what is that to me?
Let him have his day;
Yet this issue now defies a simple judgement
Such as — let him live and work —
For in truth he does more good than harm.
I am torn in my verdict,
For although he enjoys the respect and love
Of the greatest body of his students;
Tends well to his practice in this town,
And criticizes with good cause
The parasitic doctors and their servants
Who besmirch the healing arts wherever
One might travel and observe them at their craft —
Yet he inspires in dispute an element of danger
To us all — and that is most unfortunate.

HEAD OF TRIBUNAL: What is it that moves you to this gloomy turn
of mind?

THIRD MEMBER OF TRIBUNAL: Unlike you, gentlemen, I have moved
nearer to him
And his work than I was willing to admit.
I was there observing in the shadows
When defiance split the university,
And he threw the ancient books into the flames.
I noticed many cheer and applaud him in his act.
But I noticed, too, a wave of fear
Overcome the less hearty of his students
And his fellow teachers . . .
They responded within hours as fearful men
Will do—with hatred of him,
For he had moved beyond their comprehension,
And for this they could no longer tolerate
Or forgive him . . .
The world admires saints departed
From the thoroughfares of living—
But a saint still capable of voice;
Who shares the same food and sunlight

As your mother or the neighbouring cobbler,
Is a fearsome peer.
By his very being, he has savaged
The gentle life of the university
And for this we bear responsibility.
He surrounds himself with good devotees,
All admirable in their scholarship and dedication,
Yet the cries against his presence also mount
And can be heard if we but listen . . . .

Voices in angry shouts from various sources.

FIRST VOICE: Luther of medicine!

SECOND VOICE: Vagabond!

THIRD VOICE: Fool! . . . I know as much as you and more,
        Even though I cannot read or write my name!

FOURTH VOICE: Ox-head! . . . Forest ass of Einsedeln!

PARACELSUS *shouts back at his detractors.*

PARACELSUS: You! . . . Doctors and hirelings of doctors!
        You misbegotten crew of approved asses
        In the skin and garb of men!
        And you apothecaries . . . who cheat the people
        With demands of gold for foul broths
        From your filthy shops, less worthy
        Than the dish they are presented on!

A rush of bodies come at PARACELSUS *in attack, but he wards them off and sidesteps injury. The attack ends as quickly as it began.*

THIRD MEMBER OF TRIBUNAL: Of course, he rises to the challenge —
        Who would blame him?
        But is the nature of his replies to his tormentors
        Any worthier than theirs?
        The man is flawed by a raging temper —
        He creates enemies too readily . . .
        I therefore vote against his further service
        As town physician or a teacher,
        But knowing the quality and distinction of the man,
        I do so with a reservation rare for me —
        That he be made familiar with our deliberations,
        And that time be given to him to correct
        The discordancy his presence has excited!

HEAD OF TRIBUNAL: That generous and wise decision do I share.
　　　　　　A letter with our thoughts shall go to him at once.
　　　　　　As for the authority he requests as town physician,
　　　　　　That must be denied—are we agreed?

SECOND AND THIRD MEMBERS OF TRIBUNAL: Agreed!

The TRIBUNAL *rise and exit.* PARACELSUS *goes thoughtfully to where they sat and picks up paper they left, glances at it.*

PARACELSUS: Two letters reached me on that day—
　　　　　　One from the cowards who regulate the affairs of Basle;
　　　　　　The other from former students who had met in Zurich
　　　　　　And awaited me . . . .

Laughter. FRANZ *and a group of ragged but animated* STUDENTS *enter on lower level of set. They carry wine bottles, books and musical instruments. One begins to play the lute.*

FRANZ: Good news, brothers — our teacher arrives this night
　　　　　　To join us for wine and feasting,
　　　　　　For the gloomy days and illnesses of the German winter
　　　　　　Is heavy at this time upon us!

ANOTHER STUDENT: Red wine will warm his tired body
　　　　　　As a lusty, honest woman does with mine!

FRANZ *(Laughing)*:
　　　　　　You're drunk before we're gathered, Frederick!
　　　　　　Your words follow one another
　　　　　　With a sideways motion!

ANOTHER STUDENT: So did she, Franz . . . so did she!

PARACELSUS *moves happily towards the* STUDENTS, *but doesn't reach them.*

Above him, a thrashing body of a MAN *is lowered into silhouette on topmost level of set. The man is dying.*

Three DOCTORS *enter, led by an anxious* YOUTH, *who points to the dying man. One of the doctors goes up to the patient, watches him, then turns away to join his companions, who are comparing their finery in pantomime.*

PARACELSUS *(Facing his students)*:
　　　　　　For one week, I was blessed with such companions
　　　　　　As to more than compensate for all the hungers

Of my life!
We drank, ate, sang village songs
In the language and dialect of the countryside . . .
Often, our food and drink would scarce be touched
In the heat of argument on the future courses
Of our skills as men of medicine . . .
Or the turmoil of the country,
Where peasants were wakening
From their sleep of centuries
And demanding land and bread,
Which was their right, as toilers of the earth . . .
Of Luther, and the reformation
Of the wily, fatted church which long had strayed
From communion with any God . . .
Of inventors and men of vision—
Painters and skilled tellers of tales . . .
Of books and music they had heard . . .
All the joy of life, confined into one week
Free from the daily drudgery and cares
Which occupy the minds of honest men!

He moves nearer to the STUDENTS *and sits down to watch them.*

The DOCTOR *who observed the dying* MAN *on top level of stage approaches the other two* DOCTORS *and shakes their hands happily.*

FIRST DOCTOR: Good news, my learned friends —
        We have the ox of Einsedeln corralled at last!

SECOND DOCTOR: How so?

FIRST DOCTOR: While his friend, Frobenius, lies ill
        Paracelsus is carousing with hooligans in Zurich!

THIRD DOCTOR: Did he ask for another healer to attend him?

FIRST DOCTOR: He did. A messenger came
        To request my services at his bedside.
        But I said to myself — nay, better let
        Some hours pass before I make my way
        To the bookman's house . . . .
        For suppose Paracelsus gave him medication
        Out of spite — too strong for that gentle body
        To endure?
        Should I, then, be blamed

For what transpires? So I made excuses
To attend him later . . . .

With a groan, the ill MAN *dies above them.*

FIRST DOCTOR: When I did arrive, Frobenius was dead —
And whose responsibility was that?

SECOND DOCTOR: Not yours — you did wisely to delay your services.

FIRST DOCTOR: The city magistrates must hear the news at once —
They may view their wild charge in a different light
When word is out how he betrayed poor Frobenius
In carousal unbecoming a healer of the lowest order!

THIRD DOCTOR: Aye—it is time to act
Before the ass returns
From the cattle troughs of Zurich!

FIRST DOCTOR: And lest the claims against him don't suffice,
We would be wise to taunt him —
To raise such anger in the fool
That his own coarse mouth will crucify him
With the torrent of his untamed words!

SECOND DOCTOR: But how can we excite him to such fury?

FIRST DOCTOR: He burned the books of Galen—
Let us now say Galen, through some author,
Of which we have no knowledge,
Were to write a reply against Theophrastus Paracelsus . . .
And again, through means of which we have no
knowledge,
The letter were copied a hundred times over,
And posted on the walls of Basle
As a welcome notice for him!

SECOND DOCTOR: How this happened and through whom,
We have no knowledge!

FIRST DOCTOR: Oh, certainly — we are above such mischief!

THIRD DOCTOR: It is an anonymous attack that will raise
The blackest furies in that ill-bred bastard!
Away now — we have things to do —
Of which we have no knowledge!

Laughing, they exit.

The MESSENGER *enters and approaches* PARACELSUS *to give him a sheet of paper.* PARACELSUS *reads it, and rises angrily to his feet.*

Laughter in the darkness. The STUDENTS *leave, still miming a heated conversation.*

Three TRIBUNAL *members enter and take their place in level above him.*

PARACELSUS: Oh, God — first Frobenius! And now this infamy!
What hell on earth must man endure!
They are out to slander the very basis
Of my medicine—to destroy me
Both as doctor and a man!

More laughter. Hostile doctors and students now pass him, nipping at him with their words as dogs nipping at a wounded animal. Throughout their taunts, PARACELSUS *staggers towards the tribunal.*

HOSTILE STUDENT: Have you read Galen's reply to the fool
Who dares insult true genius—Theophrastus Paracelsus?

FIRST DOCTOR: No need to address him now with the dignity of a name
Call him what he is—a cacophrastus!

ANOTHER HOSTILE STUDENT: Cacophrastus — Galen writes to you.
Reads.
I doubt thou art worthy
To carry the piss-pot of Hippocrates . . .
Or give food to my swine or herd them!

SECOND DOCTOR: Hey, Cacophrastus — you look unwell,
Methinks you need a doctor!

More laughter and taunting cries of "Cacophrastus." PARACELSUS *reaches the* TRIBUNAL. *His speech is racing now, frantic.*

PARACELSUS: I petition you . . . to counsel and protect me!
The author of this sad lampoon
Is a daily listener at my lectures — a student!
I demand the body of my students be examined
For authorship of this libel!
I will suffer no more insolence
In my pursuit of further learning . . . .

HEAD OF TRIBUNAL *(Wearily)*:
Theophrastus Paracelsus — another suit
From you awaits our verdict!

SECOND MEMBER OF TRIBUNAL: You charge here the canon of
    Cathedral Liechtenfels . . .
    Had offered a hundred gulden to whoever cured him
    Of a lingering illness . . .
    You were summonsed, and did cure him
    For which he handed you six gulden. . . .

THIRD MEMBER OF TRIBUNAL: And you petition for recovery of the
    hundred gulden
    You felt is owing you.

PARACELSUS: That wealthy priest will pay his due!

SECOND MEMBER OF TRIBUNAL: What is the customary fee for treatment
    of this nature?
    Is there another medical opinion
    To enlighten us?

A doctor enters, bowing and scraping.

DOCTOR: Honoured and gracious gentlemen . . .
    Far be it for me to question the learned wisdom
    Of a peer in my profession—
    But methinks the fee provided Paracelsus
    For this treatment overpayment . . .
    I would have done as much
    For four. . . .

HEAD OF TRIBUNAL *(Irritated)*:
    Theophrastus Paracelsus —
    A petition of this nature absorbs our time
    From matters of a worthier
    And more urgent character . . .
    Perhaps you would think again
    Before you next trouble us
    With trivia of this or like importance!

PARACELSUS *glowers at them furiously.*

PARACELSUS: So you would villify the healer,
    You pompous simpletons!

HEAD OF TRIBUNAL: Enough! I order you to silence!

PARACELSUS: Order your dogs to silence—
    This is Paracelsus you address, idiot!
    The wealthy and the law judge healing

As if it were a matter of repairing shoes!
Look about you, fools!
The canon you protect was never ill . . .
I knew as much from the moment that I saw him
In his silken bed . . . it was a ruse
To trick and humiliate the principles
On which I stand! By whom?
Those you protect in your foolishness—
The healers you allow to practise in this city . . .
Murderers who burn, cut and tear human flesh
Without understanding of why or what they do!
And their servants, the apothecaries
With their compounds of rubbish . . .
You collude to destroy the brightest moment
Medicine has known yet — and for your ignorance
Neither history nor I will forgive you!

HEAD OF TRIBUNAL: I have heard enough!
Have him seized and imprisoned at once!

SECOND MEMBER OF TRIBUNAL (Rising to his feet):
Guard! Seize this man!
We will deal with this impertinence
Tomorrow morning!

Two GUARDSMEN rush in and pin the arms of PARACELSUS behind his back.
They try to lead him away, but he struggles, shouting after the departing
TRIBUNAL.

PARACELSUS (Raging):
Follow after me, Avicenna, Galen, Rhasis!
Follow you me, and not I you . . . ye from Paris.
From Montpellier . . .
From Wirtemberg . . .
From Meissen . . .
From Cologne . . .
From Vienna . . .
From the Danube, Rhine . . .
The islands of the seas . . .
Italy, Dalmatia . . . Athens . . .
Greek, Arab, Israelite . . .
Follow you me, and not I you . . .
I shall be monarch, and mine the monarchy
Which shall bind all your countries!
How will you shouters endure it

When your Cacophrastus from the dark hills
Of Einsedeln becomes prince of the monarchy
And you remain the chimney-sweeps?
O, poor soul of Galen, had he but lived
In immortal medicine and not been flung
Into hell's abyss by such as me!
Follow him who dare—until your footsteps
Take you also to the devil's fortress!

He is now pushed violently away into the wings. Over his outcry, the chant "Cacophrastus" had been building from a gathering crowd until it begins to drown out his final words.

A sudden silence as all action freezes on upper levels of set.

On lowest level, DR. WEBB *and* DR. GUZA *are seated at a table. She is reading. He is trying to stay awake.*

DR. WEBB: What's the book?

DR. GUZA: A biography of Doctor Norman Bethune.

DR. WEBB: He was the guy who went to China . . . died there, didn't he?

DR. GUZA: Yes.

DR. WEBB: People like that leave me cold.

DR. GUZA: You've no interest in remarkable men?

DR. WEBB: None whatsoever. *Smiles.* You find that strange?

DR. GUZA: No, I don't. I find it sad . . . .

She closes the book and follows him off stage.

CURTAIN

ACT II

Curtain up.

FRANZ, *gaunt and poorly dressed, stands on the topmost level of the stage, looking off to one side where the sound of barking dogs draws nearer and recedes.*

DR. WEBB *and* DR. GUZA *are bent over a table, examining a medical reference book.*

DR. WEBB: This is a careless diagnosis, Betty, I wouldn't chance it if I was you . . . .

DR. GUZA: What do I do?

DR. WEBB: Do nothing. . . . As you say, there's no apparent discomfort. In the morning, one of the high-priced doctors can have a look at the kid!

DR. GUZA: Yes—you're right.

DR. WEBB: Why don't you sneak away and catch an hour or two of sleep? I'll wake you.

DR. GUZA: I don't dare close my eyes . . . there are strange vibes playing in my head tonight!

DR. WEBB: What're you talking about?

DR. GUZA: I . . . just feel trapped . . . by my own cowardice! Marriage, children, responsibility . . . are they real, or are they things we hide behind for anonymity?

DR. WEBB *stares at her.*

DR. WEBB: You're tired . . . and I don't know what you're talking about.

DR. GUZA: I'm not sure I believe that, Patrick! A person like you can't exist and still be sane.

DR. WEBB: Has it occurred to you that I could be the only sane one around? *Grins.* Be a doll and get us some coffee!

FRANZ: Forewarned of imprisonment,
   He and I fled Basle like two thieves
   In the dead of night.
   We carried little—some manuscripts

And books he had written . . .
A few tinctures, his sword,
And what few clothes we wore.
It was one of many flights we were to make
For once the wolves were roused
They tasted death and pursued him
No matter where we stopped to rest . . . .

Dog barking suddenly comes nearer and louder. FRANZ *turns as if to flee, but a* PRIEST *and an armed* GUARD *enter. The* PRIEST *points at* FRANZ.

PRIEST: Stand, I say!
Are you the one called Franz—
Assistant to that heretic, Paracelsus?

FRANZ *(Aside)*:
He had taught me what to say at such a time.
To Priest. Nay, I am an apprentice to the village weaver.
I know nothing of the man you seek . . . .

PRIEST *(Suspicious)*:
On your word?

FRANZ: On my word!

PRIEST: If you lie, an eternity of flame
Awaits your soul in hell—
For his heresy equals that of Luther.
Of the two of them,
I would choose that Luther live . . .
It's the other one's more deadly to the faith!
To Guard. Proceed! We must find
And drive him from this town!

They exit.

FRANZ *picks up a small bundle and jumps to lower level of stage, where he stirs a sleeping* PARACELSUS.

FRANZ: We should leave, Theophrastus, before the morning light.
Men at arms accompany the priest . . . .

PARACELSUS: At last, the true face of the holy faith!
The cudgel and the cross!

FRANZ: They speak of you as the Luther of medicine . . . .

PARACELSUS: Luther, indeed! . . . I've never met the man . . .
   Puts on his boots. But I distrust his sobriety . . .
   He has the qualities that tyranny embodies
   In her icy portrait; We Germans
   Make poor champions in the cause of truth —
   Humourless and over-dedicated,
   We sack old systems of philosophy and order
   And in their place, erect the new —
   More fearsome and less human than the old!

FRANZ: Hurry!

PARACELSUS: Perhaps, with such captors, it would be
   A worthy end, for Luther and myself
   To die within their flames!

FRANZ *stares at him with alarm.* PARACELSUS *laughs and dismisses the
remark as a bad joke.*

PARACELSUS: Nay, nay . . . do not blanch
   As a widow in the presence of a stallion!
   I do not yet contemplate my death —
   But should I do so, it would be
   At the hands of worthier foes
   Than an idiotic village priest
   And his illiterate cousin doctor!

FRANZ: Your arguments mean nothing
   In this place!

PARACELSUS *(Contemplates his shoe):*
   The down upon my chin
   Knows more than all their writers;
   My shoebuckles are more learned doctors
   Than their Galen and Avicenna,
   And all their syphilitic priests
   That spy and pry throughout their universities —
   And for this we are fugitives,
   Hounded by common dogs
   And brutish men with clubs!

FRANZ: Hurry, Theophrastus!

PARACELSUS *(Rising):*
   God will make other doctors
   Who will understand—even all the wisdom
   Of the magic arts — the very mention of which now

Is as vinegar to their throats,
Or cataracts upon their eyes!
And when that happens, lad—
Who will then redden the thin lips
Of their wives, and wipe their sharp little noses,
Unaccustomed as they are, to the smell of human toil?
The devil with a hunger napkin, that's who!
Gather my books and what is left of all my life and work —
We move onwards once again as shadows into night . . . .

FRANZ *quickly collects Paracelsus' belongings and leaves, but* PARACELSUS *hesitates.*

The WOMAN-ANGEL *enters on top level of set. She is dressed in a costume that is oddly contemporary.*

Sound of the bells of Einsedeln in far background.

PARACELSUS: Yet again . . . and for eternity,
The bones and dust of me recall
The living and the dying . . . .

WOMAN-ANGEL: You may yet relive it all as it once was;
The warmth and cold . . .
The touching of a desperate hand . . .
The fumes and scalding acids of your chemistry . . .
The odours and the silent plea
Of a dying woman begging through her eyes
To save her life, and spare her children
The agony of living orphans. . . .

PARACELSUS *shudders visibly.*

PARACELSUS: They still die in such a way?

WOMAN-ANGEL: They do . . . and to the last gasp,
Hoping for a healer with miracles
In his enchanted hands and brain!

PARACELSUS: You taunt me, devil!
Inhuman suffering cries out
For super-human healing—
The impossible curatives
Must be applied, even when death
Has stepped between the healer
And the stricken!

Patients are being led and carried past him. He moves among them, administering and comforting.

PARACELSUS: My skills . . . my very will to live,
   Must transmute my spirit and my tissue
   Into health and life within the patient.
   Then I rejoice, for the harmony of life
   And change has moved another mountain
   From the sacred human skull!

A distressed COUPLE *lead two* MEN *carrying a young* GIRL *on a pallet towards* PARACELSUS. *At sight of the doctor, the* MOTHER *turns away.*

MOTHER: The priest did say he was a wizard
   And in truth, he is . . .
   The girl will die, I tell you,
   Spare her from dying
   In the devil's hands!

FATHER: I cannot! Be he God or devil,
   It is the same to me — the child must live!
   To Paracelsus. Help me!
   My only daughter . . . has never taken step
   From birth!

PARACELSUS *deftly uncovers the legs of the* GIRL *and examines them. As he does so, he turns to the* MOTHER.

PARACELSUS: Why the darkness in your face, woman?

MOTHER: Don't speak to me as an equal—
   I am a simple woman. If God chooses
   I should suffer—I am content
   With such attention!

PARACELSUS: This child is the work of God, as well . . . .

MOTHER: Speak not His name to me!
   The flames of hell
   Burn within your eyes!

FATHER: Hush, woman! He is our final hope!

PARACELSUS *covers the girl's legs.*

PARACELSUS: Her legs are healthy, as your own!

MOTHER: They are withered! Daily she dies!
   What sort of fool are you?

PARACELSUS *(Sharply)*:
> Speak no more of dying
> In her presence! Methinks the cradle of your love
> Is damp and dismal as a pauper's grave!
> Has song and laughter ever cheered
> The hours of her sleep?

MOTHER: We pray, as Christians must!
> It is a sacrilege to sing
> When illness, like a hungry dog,
> Never leaves our door!

PARACELSUS *speaks to the* CHILD.

PARACELSUS: There is a river nearby — can you hear
> The murmur of the waters?

GIRL: Yes—it is like a wind
> Blowing through the garden!

PARACELSUS *takes a piece of paper and fashions a boat out of it.*

PARACELSUS: This river flows into other rivers,
> Which in turn, empty into stormy oceans
> Where giant fish and reptiles
> Pit their strength against the raging winds
> And lashing tides. . . .

GIRL: Even as you speak, I can see high waves
> Such as would wash these hills
> Clean of homes, churches, markets;
> And all people who work, worship,
> And inhabit them!
> Have you seen all of which you speak?

PARACELSUS: Yes—and a great yearning overtakes me
> For communion once more with strength
> That is greater than my own.
> But I need help . . . .

The GIRL *lifts her head from the pallet and stares quizzically at him.*

GIRL: What help is it that you need?

PARACELSUS: I want you to rise and walk with me
> Towards the river, so that together,
> Good friends can bid farewell
> To this frail toy—a gentle sacrifice

In memory of a summer evening
When lindens whispered, and the river did invite
A young girl and a tired man
To think beyond themselves—
Of meadows, storms and the mighty muscled sea!

PARACELSUS *steps back. The* GIRL *rises, trembling, to a sitting position.*
PARACELSUS *beckons her to her feet. She takes a painful step forward and*
falls into his arms.

The FATHER *leaps forward, overjoyed, and takes the girl into his embrace.*

FATHER: She walks—oh, God! My child walks!
What is your fee for this miracle, doctor?

PARACELSUS: There is no fee — you are as poor as I.
But if you have some bread, I would share it
With you . . . Franz and I
Have not eaten for two days.

The MOTHER *reluctantly takes a small loaf from her satchel, breaks part of*
it off, and drops it at the feet of PARACELSUS. *Then she crosses herself, and*
supporting her child, hurries the father and girl away.

PARACELSUS *stares at the bread before him, then bending down, picks it up.*

The WOMAN-ANGEL *laughs bitterly. There are tears in his eyes as*
PARACELSUS *looks up at her.*

PARACELSUS: Why do you laugh? At human frailty?
It is a dream . . . nothing more . . .
I am vapour now . . . four hundred years of age.
Still I tremble at the thought . . .
Of finding God beyond forbidden doors!

WOMAN-ANGEL: Fool! You are as lonely as a speck of dust
Frozen in the cosmos!
Where now, is the king,
Whom you served with such distinction?

She exits. PARACELSUS *thoughtfully chews on the crust of bread.*

PARACELSUS: Christ made the healing of sick minds and bodies
His paramount preoccupation—
I cannot do less than follow
His example . . . *Smiles.*
I praise the Spanish doctor,
For he does not go about like an idle fellow,

64

Finely dressed in velvet . . .
He wears clothes of leather
And an apron on which to wipe his hands . . . .

A BEGGAR *comes past, holding out his hand.* PARACELSUS *gives him the remainder of the bread. Then* PARACELSUS *examines his smock, which is stained.*

PARACELSUS: The stains upon this smock
Are a badge of my profession . . .
I was proud of every stain and burn
Upon my clothes, for these were
A diary of my treatments . . . .

FRANZ *appears in a separate playing area. He is carrying paper, a quill and inkwell. Sitting down, he writes.*

FRANZ: They were pygmies as compared to him —
These men who drove him from the city
And hunted him like some deranged animal
Through the villages and towns . . . .

PARACELSUS: I do not fear them, but I do fear
The discredit they may do my works . . .
For there are always scholars
Who will defend the braying of an ass
When it issues from a soft, well-shaven mouth!

FRANZ: We fled from town to town . . .
In Ensisheim we stopped,
For he desired to see a meteor
Which fell to earth a year before his birth . . . .

PARACELSUS *turns and touches a stone in the set behind him.* A PRIEST *enters.*

FRANZ: He examined it — touched it, and exclaimed . . . .

PARACELSUS: It is made of stone and iron, Franz!
And it weighs a hundred and ten pounds!

PRIEST: You are wrong, stranger . . .
The components of the meteor
Are known only to the Lord!
And its weight is equal to the weight
Of the three sturdiest men
In this principality!

The PRIEST *makes the sign of the cross over the meteor.* PARACELSUS *laughs.*

PARACELSUS: My studies lead me to believe
        The universe is one creation!
        There is nothing in the cosmos
        That is foreign to this earth!

PRIEST: What nonsense you prattle at your age!
        Have you grown carrots on the moon — eh?
        This is a virtuous town you visit,
        With short temper for your insolence!

PARACELSUS *laughs again, nudges the severe* PRIEST *in the ribs in the fashion of a countryman. The* PRIEST *recoils, and rubs the place clean where* PARACELSUS *touched his robes.*

PARACELSUS: Tell me then, cowherd of the soul,
        What is this stone?

PRIEST: It is a stone of heaven
        Possessing secrets no man should understand!
        It fell to earth on such a night
        As still throws fear into the aged of this town . . .
        A night of wild lightning and deafening thunder —
        And then the stone, like a flaming arrow,
        Fell beside the city gates . . . .

PARACELSUS: And then it stood up, and asked directions
        To the church!

PRIEST: Nay, Nay! . . . When it had cooled
        We rolled it on a pallet,
        And eight virtuous men carried it
        With the dignity becoming such a miracle,
        To the church!
        By now, the storm had passed,
        And people of the town, even to the infants,
        Gathered in the square to sing psalms
        To this miracle the eight men brought
        Amongst them!
        Bow with me now, stranger,
        And let us pray before it!

PARACELSUS: Go christen you some children, fool—
        Who, still not possessed of language,
        Are lulled by the cadence of your voice.

You bore me, as a nightingale in time,
Bores a drowsy man . . . .

He yawns. The PRIEST *angers.*

PRIEST: We did not invite you here
To scoff at what our Lord,
In the bounty of His wisdom,
Left us as reminder of His awesome grace!
Begone! For you appear in your dress and swagger
As a ruffian, or a thief of horses!

PARACELSUS *gestures derisively at the* PRIEST *and both men part. The* PRIEST *exits.*

PARACELSUS *moves towards* FRANZ, *who hands him a page of notes.*

FRANZ: These are the ailments I treated
In the town last night—
And an inventory of our medications.

PARACELSUS *studies the notes briefly, then smiles.*

PARACELSUS: You have a habit, Franz,
For using Latin names for ailments
In a German body!
I knew a poet in Bavaria,
Who wrote his thoughts in Greek,
Believing this gave them dignity
And elevation!

FRANZ: I do feel that in medicine and in gentler arts,
German is a minor tongue . . . .

PARACELSUS: What a strange judgement you place
On the German word . . . and on yourself!

FRANZ: How so, Theophrastus?

PARACELSUS: A man who trades his language
Might in time trade his home and motherland
For valueless refinements . . .
Do not let the edicts of some mighty, distant empire
Rule your thoughts, *or how you speak them!*
That is the first threshold you must cross
On the rugged road to freedom . . .
Be a Greek or Lithuanian, Magyar or a Turk . . .
Whatever womb your mother bore you from—
Be that first!

FRANZ: But in medicine . . . .

PARACELSUS: Is mystery?

FRANZ: To the common people—yes!

PARACELSUS: Medicine, above all else—must nevermore
　　　　Be closeted in secrecy,
　　　　Either in language or its truths
　　　　From the common man and woman—
　　　　For as healing rises from the people
　　　　So must it be given back to people!
　　　　The healer understanding this
　　　　Has reached the first plateau
　　　　Of nobility among the human species!

They are interrupted by a noise of jangling chains. A demented MAN *is led onstage, chained at the ankles, wrists and throat. He is naked to the waist, gleaming with perspiration. As he is brought to* PARACELSUS, *he is dancing insanely.*

ESCORT: Can you do something for him, doctor, before he
　maddens our village?

PARACELSUS *rushes to the man, inspects his eyes and mouth.*

FRANZ *retreats and continues writing.*

PARACELSUS: How long has he been thus?

ESCORT: One week the spell has been upon him—
　　　　He has neither slept nor eaten,
　　　　But has broken dishes, trampled his garden
　　　　Into dust — alarmed his wife and children . . . .

PARACELSUS: Enough! Bring me a musician
　　　　Who knows the lively airs of country dancing!
　　　　Unchain him—he is not a beast!

The ESCORT *unchains the demented man and runs off stage. Paracelsus soothes the man with cooing sounds, stroking his chest and cheeks with gentle motions of his hands.*

The bells of Einsedeln begin to peal in far background.

A moment later, A FIDDLER *is brought on stage by the* ESCORT, *who moves back from the jerking man.*

PARACELSUS *turns to the* MUSICIAN.

PARACELSUS: Watch my hands—and play in time
    To my gestures!

The MUSICIAN *lifts the fiddle and begins playing his instrument to the conducting of* PARACELSUS, *who never takes his eyes off the demented man. The tune is in time to the rhythms of the possessed man.*

Slowly, PARACELSUS *slows the rhythm of the music. The spasms of the patient also slow with the change in tempo of the music. The pacing becomes slower and slower, until at last it stops.*

The PATIENT *stands wearily, swaying from side to side, the spasms now ended, his head drooping. He falls forward and is caught by* PARACELSUS.

PARACELSUS *(To Escort and Musician)*:
    Take him home — the man is wasted with fatigue.
    He will sleep a day or two,
    And when he wakes, give him food and this —
    Hands Escort a small satchel of medication.
    It will prolong his sleep,
    And when he wakes the second time,
    He will not recall
    This painful interlude.

ESCORT: The devils that possessed him — where are they?

PARACELSUS *(Gently)*:
    There are no devils, brother — only pain.

ESCORT: No — there are devils in a man possessed!

PARACELSUS: Then I have freed the devils
    And they have gone in pursuit
    Of better things to do — go now!
    The man needs rest from his ordeal. . . .

The ESCORT *and* MUSICIAN *carry the sleeping patient out.*

Bells of Einsedeln continue tolling.

PARACELSUS *packs his manuscripts and laboratory supplies and fastens his cloak around himself.*

DR. WEBB *and* DR. GUZA *check out some surgical supplies on lowest level of set.*

DR. WEBB: . . .And then this sonofabitch pulls out in front of me in one of those one-man European cars. So ecology or not, I'm one of those fellows, Betty, who wants plenty of steel around me when I join my fellow humans on the freeway!

DR. GUZA: You're afraid of dying?

DR. WEBB: What sort of question is that? Sure I'm afraid of getting killed stupidly . . . aren't you?

DR. GUZA: I don't know . . . I suppose it depends on whether one dies stupidly . . . or just . . . dies.

DR. WEBB: Alright, then . . . *any* death is stupid in this business. And until I hear otherwise, I'm gonna live with that and not worry about deeper meanings to things. Let's pack this stuff up!

FRANZ: Where do we travel now?

PARACELSUS: To Esslingen . . . where my family of Hohenheim
Still have the relics of a family home.
There is a cellar in the garden . . .
Where I have much to do . . .
You may leave once you have moved me there . . . .

FRANZ: Am I no longer useful to you?

The WOMAN-ANGEL *appears on top of highest stage elevation. A few peasants wander past her, cowering in her presence, but she watches* PARACELSUS.

The bells stop.

PARACELSUS: I have now reached the limits of my scrutiny
Of illness in its myriad forms . . .
And explorations of the cures of tinctures, salves,
Purgatives and essences which abound
In earth, rock and atmosphere . . .
I must now search for the secrets of Christ Himself;
In the cures he wrought, even through the soil
Of the grave . . .
There is something which defies me . . .
Dazzling my eyes as lightning —
Lashing at my back as an autumn rain —
I feel, what wisdom I have gained is but a flicker
Of a candle in the centre of a vast,
Enshrouded sea . . . .

The WOMAN-ANGEL *laughs.*

FRANZ: I beg to stay with you.

PARACELSUS: If I loved you less, the answer would be — yes!
But it is a dark and dangerous thing I do —

> For I must move into the realms of magic —
> Of necromancy—the unspoken horrors
> Of the opening grave . . . . Incantations, if need be . . .
> And the influence of tides, moon and stars
> On human health and destiny.
> In short—someone must sift the soil
> Of the devil's garden, for perchance
> Some unknown healing truth is buried there!

The WOMAN-ANGEL *laughs again.* FRANZ *shudders.*

FRANZ *(Bitterly)*:
> So I am now unfit to work in any
> But the safest surgery!

PARACELSUS: I am an aging man — I have no fear . . .
> The path I take may lead me to the gallows,
> Or death upon the flaming stake as heretic . . .
> As a disciple of the devil . . .
> Against that, Franz, even my great name
> Is no defence—I fear for you!

PARACELSUS *scowls at* FRANZ, *who meets his gaze steadily.* PARACELSUS *turns suddenly and exits. The* WOMAN-ANGEL *also vanishes in the direction he has taken.*

Over FRANZ'S *lines,* PARACELSUS *reappears in another, lower elevation of the stage. He now wears a doublet, a furred cap, and a gold chain with a jewel around his neck. In a recessed area of set, he installs a small furnace and a crucible. A peasant helper of limited intelligence brings him a wooden table, on which* PARACELSUS *takes out paper and writing pens from his satchel.*

FRANZ: Our destination was a damp, abandoned cellar,
> Scarce larger than a prison cell . . .
> We arrived by night, for Theophrastus
> Was now a furtive man . . . setting out his laboratory
> In a strange and innovative way . . . some underground,
> Some above . . . Seldom did we eat, and never rested . . .
> Working like a man possessed — his eyes glowed
> And sank within his skull . . . The habit of his dress
> More that of magician than a doctor . . . .
> This man bore less and less resemblance
> To the healer of a year ago
> Than a raven to a frightened dog!

FRANZ *moves to* PARACELSUS, *igniting the light below the crucible.*

PARACELSUS: How often will this scene replay itself —
        To terrorize and fascinate the Christian soul?
        To Franz. Melt me lead within that crucible
        Then turn your face towards the wall—
        And I'll transmute the lead into the purest gold for you!

FRANZ *is startled and turns quickly to face* PARACELSUS, *who is chuckling.*

FRANZ: You jest with me . . . do you not?

PARACELSUS: Ah, so even you believe such foolishness—
        What chance then has my reputation
        To survive what flacks will say about these nights?

FRANZ: There is no harm in what I see you do!

PARACELSUS: You see nothing. . . .
        Where we are settled now is foreign ground
        To men of studied grace and learning.
        Astrology is still the art of demons,
        But its courses are too frequently exact
        To be dismissed.

FRANZ: I feel no fear, why should you th—

PARACELSUS: You are a braver man than I, lad . . .
        For I confess I am afraid.
        Did you decipher the cabalistic characters
        I left with you last night?

FRANZ: No.

PARACELSUS: We will examine them again. Go to the roof . . .
        Compare this cart to the position of the stars —
        And take you careful note of moon to Mars.

Taking paper and quill, FRANZ *exits.*

WOMAN-ANGEL *enters on a higher level and hovers over* PARACELSUS *at his work.*

WOMAN-ANGEL: As once before, I have informed them
        Of your works!

PARACELSUS *stares hard at her.*

PARACELSUS: Who?

WOMAN-ANGEL: My primitives, who fly to fear,
　　　　As moths to flame!

PARACELSUS *shrugs angrily.*

PARACELSUS: Keep them from me, or I
　　　　Will end this exercise!

WOMAN-ANGEL *looks lovingly at him.*

WOMAN-ANGEL: You will end nothing, doctor.
　　　　The course of your enquiry . . .
　　　　As well as time of your birth and death,
　　　　Is as set as the pattern and movement
　　　　Of the stars you scan each night!
　　　　I promised you surprises
　　　　In a different age and time . . . .
　　　　You choose instead, the folly
　　　　Of a noble and a misspent life. . . .
　　　　I cannot save you now. . . . Your doom
　　　　Is sealed by fools and hooligans.
　　　　Farewell, sweet healer—I will return
　　　　To celebrate your death!

She moves back from him and disappears into gloom. Three hooded THUGS
pass on highest elevation, armed with cudgels, their empty faces turned to
PARACELSUS *as they pass.*

PARACELSUS *stares blankly at his notes, and a shudder passes through his*
body.

PARACELSUS: It is strange, how fear
　　　　As ancient as a suffocating dream
　　　　Still grips me with an icy claw . . .
　　　　I still might have withdrawn . . .
　　　　Returned to some obscure practice
　　　　Of my healing skills within a drowsy town;
　　　　Bathed in a glow of gratitude and fame —
　　　　And yet penniless and hungry—I
　　　　Entertain the devil for one purpose—
　　　　I must *know*!
　　　　God—please help and guide me!
　　　　For I do not understand your ways
　　　　With man!

FRANZ *enters at a run.*

FRANZ: Theophrastus—they are at the door!
      Asking to see you now!

PARACELSUS: Who?

FRANZ: The devil's own servants, it would seem
      From their dress and the strange mutterings
      They make!

PARACELSUS: Then send them home to the devil—I have no time
      To entertain the idiocy of fools and pranksters!

FRANZ *turns to leave, but his path is blocked by the entry of three hooded figures with strange mystic designs on their long robes.* FRANZ *is alarmed.*

FRANZ: My God—they have forced the door!

LEADER OF GROUP: Welcome to our town, great healer
      And Philosopher!
      We had an omen during secret meetings
      Informing us of your arrival!

PARACELSUS *(Surprised by their costuming)*:
      Who in hell's name are you?
      State your business and be gone!

LEADER OF GROUP *(Fawning now)*:
      It was wise of me to place a portion
      Of my robe into the door when this callow youth
      Tried to shut us out! Never fear, Paracelsus,
      We are real, influential and of the true conversion.

PARACELSUS: What?

LEADER OF GROUP: But you have doubtless had a different story
      From . . . this boy.
      I would dismiss him now
      And send him on his way. . . .
      We can provide you with a trusting servant,
      Sworn to secrecy and such obedience
      Your every wish, no matter how strange
      Or possibly repugnant to him,
      Would be as the wishes guiding his own spirit!

PARACELSUS *(Laughs)*:
      Oft-times I feel my lack of rest
      Plays wonder with my eyes and ears . . .
      Is it the same with you, Franz?

FRANZ: Aye . . . last night I dreamed of flying turtles.

LEADER *of the group is miffed now.*

LEADER OF GROUP: I am a forerunner of the militia crucifera Angelica,
As well as magistrate in town—
So you are well protected here!

SECOND MEMBER OF GROUP: And I am of the brotherhood of mystic
Numerology—
Keeper of the largest inn—where food and lodging
Are available to you at moment's notice.

THIRD MEMBER OF GROUP: I am a magician of the darker arts,
Well versed in exorcism;
Curses, which inflect great harm
On enemies and . . . .

PARACELSUS *glares at them.*

PARACELSUS: What are you to me, or I to you?

LEADER OF GROUP *(To Group)*:
It is the boy — I like him not . . . .
I see he will cause dissension. . . .
To Paracelsus. Our brotherhoods are strong
And influential—we will protect you,
But in return, we ask—only as a gesture
Of our mutual understanding—that you share
Your secrets of the mystic arts with us.

PARACELSUS: Secrets? — What secrets?
Did you think that God has placed
Eternal blinders on the eyes of men?

They glance uncertainly at one another. Something is not as they had expected.

PARACELSUS *(Curious)*:
What secrets do you wish
Me to bestow on you?

LEADER OF GROUP: The secret of power — how to alter minds
Of prince or duke, to influence appointments
Either from our ranks, or favourable
To our cause.

PARACELSUS: I see. . . . *To Second Member* . . . And you?

SECOND MEMBER OF GROUP: The same. . . .
For our brothers crave respect,
Since ours is the one and final truth of prophecy
And dominion over human frailty!

PARACELSUS *turns to* THIRD MEMBER. THIRD MEMBER *hesitates and is nervous.*

PARACELSUS: Well?

THIRD MEMBER OF GROUP: It is said by many . . .
You possess the secret
Of transmuting lead to gold. . . .
I would give the fingers of my hands
For the secret of that trick!

PARACELSUS *unbuckles the belt around his waist and holds it threateningly.*

PARACELSUS *(Roaring)*:
Aye . . . I possess that secret!
And others so fearsome, the very heart of a witness
To my dark and magic arts would break with terror!
With a gesture of my hand heavenwards, as thus,
I can cause deafening thunder and such deluge
Of rain and hail as would sweep your town
Into the river!

Loud crack of thunder from outside. FRANZ *and three members of* GROUP *jump with surprise and alarm.*

PARACELSUS: With a glance of eye, I can cause a man
Of splendid health to clutch his throat and scream
With pain so agonizing, the veins within his head
Would swell and burst, and all who saw his suffering
Would be struck dumb for eternity!
I can summon devils, angels. . . .

Misshapen forms of people enter and pass on either side of them. Members of the GROUP *cringe away.* FRANZ *is bewildered.*

PARACELSUS: The earth to rise and break within
The graveyard, releasing groaning skulls—
Still gnawed by dripping worms . . . to shriek
In a hollow wind of voice . . . .

Passing misshapen people give life to his words.

PARACELSUS: Paracelsus . . . .

PASSING MAN: King of magic!

PASSING WOMAN: Let us be, for you are stronger . . . .

PASSING MAN: Than the strongest devil. . . .

PASSING CROWD *(In unison)*:
    We succumb!

In grotesque postures of torment, they flee the stage.

PARACELSUS *lays about him with his belt, over the backs and buttocks of the three members of mystic group.*

PARACELSUS: Furthermore, as you will witness now,
    I can, with well placed strokes
    Of my belt across the arses of the scum
    Of basest greed, ignorance and infamy . . .
    Cause its disciples to scatter,
    Mrahwing like a pack of alley cats!

Covering their heads, the three scatter in confusion.

LEADER *of the group turns, angered and humilated.*

LEADER OF GROUP: You cannot bear more enemies, Paracelsus!
    It's unwise of you to handle us this way—
    Our anger will bring you to account for this!
    We will not announce the hour or location
    Of our vengeance, but look you to your safety now
    Each moment of the night and day!

PARACELSUS *glowers at him in a terrifying way. Raising his arms like an attacking hawk, he rushes at them, causing them to retreat, stumbling and tripping over one another.*

PARACELSUS: Threaten me, would you? . . . Harrh!

After the group has fled, PARACELSUS *breaks into jubilant laughter.* FRANZ *also laughs with relief.*

PARACELSUS: What strange bedfellows have our studies brought us!
    Grown men, with painted bedspreads
    Wrapped around their bodies, like some
    Weathercocks of China! Hoods upon
    Their heads, like the beaks of drowsy magpies . . .
    Even witchcraft has lost what dignity it had!
    Mimics. . . . I am a magistrate, oh noble healer!
    And I the keeper of an inn . . . But me —

I am the lowest devil of the trio —
I am just a common thief . . . Help me make gold
Out of common shit — and for this I'll give you
All the fingers of my hands! *Laughs.*
What could I do with his fingers?
Threat them on a string and wear them
'Round my neck?

Sound of the bells of Einsedeln.

FRANZ: I am now afraid, Theophrastus!

PARACELSUS: A man is known for his works, his friends . . .
The good he does — but a man is also known
For the stature of his enemies!

FRANZ: They will be back . . . you know they will be back!
With violence more cruel and stealthy
That that of pompous doctors and of priests!

PARACELSUS *goes to his burning forge.*

PARACELSUS: Then I will fight them with their weapons, Franz.

Making a rapid gesture over the forge with his hand, the furnace flares with white, phosphorescent flame, then dies down. PARACELSUS *takes the crucible in tongs and turns swiftly, holding it out to* FRANZ.

PARACELSUS *(Frowning, urgent):*
Remember well, Franz,
What I did ask you to prepare
Within this crucible!

FRANZ: A balm of zinc and heavy oils for the treatment
Of skin ailments peculiar to milkmaids. . . .

PARACELSUS: And what is it I hold before you now?

FRANZ *stares into the crucible. Rubs his eyes with disbelief.*

FRANZ: No! . . . It is not possible.

PARACELSUS: What is it you see?

FRANZ: A crucible of the purest gold!

PARACELSUS *laughs and replaces the crucible over the flames.*

PARACELSUS: It might do to trick some greedy landlord
When next we lack money for our rent!

FRANZ: That *was* gold! I know the properties of gold
For I have often worked with it!
That was no trick, Theophrastus — or was it?

PARACELSUS *looks at him enigmatically.*

PARACELSUS: Certainly, it was gold — what other answer do you seek?
It dazzles fools—bewilders scholars —
Confounds kings — if such be the influence of gold
Then it was gold!

PARACELSUS *laughs bitterly and turns his back on* FRANZ.

Bells stop.

PARACELSUS *returns to his observations at the forge and to his writing.*

FRANZ *is pained, looks at* PARACELSUS *a long moment, then turns to the audience.*

PARACELSUS *(Harshly)*:
There is nothing in the stars!
It is in the human wisdom that the secrets lie!

FRANZ: The signs of his later torment
Were already there . . . in his twisted fingers
And his swollen hands . . .
The stoop of back . . .
The loss of hair and teeth . . .
He now treated patients often without surgery
Or drugs — and I rejoiced and shuddered
At the miracles he workd. . . .

PARACELSUS: Don't look pained or startled, Franz . . .
The patient's will to live is a potent medicine —
Despair and gloom are hand-maidens
To the monarchy of death . . .
Recognize the pain created of the heart and mind,
And prescribe from your own spirit
An antidote of joy and love so dazzling
It radiates like flame from your hands and eyes!
This, and the words you choose to speak
Are miracles of healing created
In a true physician's presence.
If you are incapable of such sacrifice
Of wisdom, spirit and yourself,
Go then into commerce or the priesthood,
For of a doctor you will only be a hollow sham!

FRANZ *lowers his head in pain.*

FRANZ: Why do I merit such anger and contempt?

PARACELSUS *turns to him, his expression pained.*

PARACELSUS: Don't whimper like a lowlands maiden!
        I speak my mind openly to you, as to a son . . . .

FRANZ: A son can be hurt by a thoughless father!

PARACELSUS: *Hurt?* Look at me, wretch!
        There is nothing theoretic in my teaching of you;
        Everything I say I *know,* because I've *lived* it!
        Listen to the hearts of things
        Not the spoken or the written word alone!

FRANZ: Although I love you much, Theophrastus,
        I am a man of reason — I weigh
        Your arguments against the lesser ones
        Of your opponents.

PARACELSUS (*Angry now*):
        Words devoid of passion
        Are nothing — mere ashes in the wind
        Of distant fires. . . .
        I was a lad on my way to school . . . .
        My mother led me to the bridge
        On the river Sihl, which flowed
        Beside our home. . . .
        The water in the river boiled and roared . . .
        I heard not her words, but in her eyes
        I saw her love and last farewell . . .
        As if shrieked from the very edge of hell!
        And then . . . in her madness, she dove
        Into the river, her body breaking open
        On the rocks below the bridge like some
        Fragile vessel of the darkest, sacred wine . . .
        In seconds, the plumes of churning water
        Reddened with her blood as far as I could see . . .

FRANZ *covers his face in his hands.*

FRANZ: No!

PARACELSUS: I howled my love for her . . .
        She was my mother, who had but an hour before

Wakened me from sleep, prepared for me a bowl
Of barley gruel with oil . . .
Dusted my satchel . . .
Combed my hair. . . .

FRANZ: No Theophrastus—I have heard enough!

PARACELSUS *begins to talk rapidly, as if deranged momentarily with the memory.*

PARACELSUS: I watched the river wash her foaming blood
Towards the sea —
And remembered, as a dying man remembers birth . . .
She left me as an infant by the road
Which passed our house . . .
My father gone to tend to patients
In the town;
I was alone, when some soldiers,
Dark and snarling with diseases of the mind
Came by and saw me.
They removed the cloth around my loins,
And baring swords and daggers,
Amused themselves by cutting at my penis
As they had seen in Palestine
Done to Jewish lads in circumcision. . . .
Tiring of the sport and my shrieks of pain,
They left me there, unwrapped and bleeding. . . .
I tried to draw myself into the house,
But before I reached the door . . . a wild boar,
Maddened by the scent of blood, came charging
From the woods.
He closed his steaming jaws around my wound,
And with jerking actions of his head,
Tore away my manhood and ran grunting
Down the road — masticating penis,
Testicles and strings of pale fibre
Torn from out my body. . . .

FRANZ: *(Weeping)*:
Merciful God!

PARACELSUS *(Softly now)*:
Look gently when you look on pain,
My student — it is not the duty of humanity to suffer.
But only if you understand all suffering

Can you comprehend the meaning
Of a healer's obligation.

FRANZ: Then let me suffer as you suffered—
I am not afraid!

PARACELSUS: You will suffer, have no fear.
So do not whimper when you hunger,
Or the colour leaves your cheeks
For lack of sleep—
That is the pain of pampered dandies,
So break it in your nature now.
We have more lofty undertakings.
This is but an interlude.

The bells go silent.

PARACELSUS: Go tend your observations —
We have lost two hours of this night . . . .

DR. GUZA *and* DR. WEBB *are seated at the table on the lowest level of set, poring through medical journals.*

DR. WEBB: Look at this — ads and more ads from the drug industry. I feel that when I grow up an' become a big boy, ninety percent of my medical practice will consist of dispensing chemicals which I've never seen and know nothing about!

DR. GUZA *(Laughing)*: Doctor Patrick Webb, P.F.P.I. . . . pusher for the pharmaceutics industry!

DR. WEBB: I only hope somebody up there knows what the hell's going on. I don't.

DR. GUZA: And think of what happens when a breakthrough is made in cancer and heart diseases! The ranks of the unemployed will swell by thousands!

DR. WEBB: How come?

DR. GUZA: What will happen to all the careers dedicated to worrying about cancer and heart sufferers?

DR. WEBB: They'll promote some new disease! How about promoting mental illness to the hungry? Or nuclear weapons to the starving of the Orient?

DR. GUZA *stops laughing.*

DR. GUZA: That's not funny, Patrick!

DR. WEBB: Then so much for your faith in human goodness — theirs or ours! I think the world stinks, honey — and I want no part of it!

DR. GUZA: But you're a doctor!

DR. WEBB: What the hell does that mean? Words like love, freedom, pity—have all been turned to shit by this! *Angrily points to an advertisement in the journal.* So if I want to live, I've got to play the game—I'm a businessman, and screw your Schwietzers and Bethunes! In the operating theatre, I'll be as good as any of them. Outside the hospital — who gives a damn anyway?

They glower at each other, then return to their reading.

PARACELSUS *is at his laboratory, setting up experiments and making hurried notes.* FRANZ *moves away from him, speaks to the audience.*

FRANZ: The world needed a new birth, he told me once . . .
            I did not understand his statement.

PARACELSUS: All created things are by their nature
            Hostile to men, and men to them. . . .
            Why, I cannot answer — for that is the nature
            And tragedy of human destiny
            Beneath this canopy of heaven
            And its mysteries!

FRANZ: At times he frightened me
            With his suspended logic. . . .

PARACELSUS: If God works a miracle, He does it through people!
            In healing illness, He does it through the doctor . . . .
            And in this, there are two doctors;
            Those who heal with medicine,
            And those who heal as if by miracle.
            I have done both, and do observe
            That God accomplishes through a physician
            A transmutation in the patient,
            Should he will to live . . .
            Yet medicine itself does not belong to faith
            But to the sight of questioning and agnostic eyes.

FRANZ: He spoke to me of Asia,
            And theories he had heard
            From healers there . . . .

PARACELSUS: A man is his own doctor,
        Helping nature to provide the needs
        Of his body and his mind. . . .
        All things are in the inner
        As they are in the outer world —
        Our wounds heal from within outwards
        As nature heals itself and levels out the hollows
        Of scars and injury —
        Heaven and earth, air and water
        Are a man . . . And a man is a world
        With heaven and earth, air and water —
        When we administer medicine,
        We administer this entire world
        To him. . . .

A sound of tramping feet. Six hooded FIGURES *appear over top level of set. The* LEADING FIGURE *carries a silver cross, the others carry staves and torches.*

The LEADING FIGURE *sees* PARACELSUS *and points.*

LEADING FIGURE: There he is — Lucifer himself!

On signal, they rush down and surround PARACELSUS *and* FRANZ. FRANZ *is fearful, but* PARACELSUS *slowly puts away his manuscripts into a satchel, buckles on his sword.*

LEADING FIGURE: Are you the one they call Paracelsus, the healer?

PARACELSUS *ignores him.*

LEADING FIGURE: For if you are, then do you confess
        With consorting with witches and the dead?
        Evoking devils and creating magic
        Through evil stars? . . . Answer me!

PARACELSUS *continues to ignore him.*

LEADING FIGURE *is becoming disconcerted. Points to the laboratory equipment.*

LEADING FIGURE: Are these the tools of your evil arts?

ANOTHER MAN: He is struck dumb
        By the cross you carry!
        Wave it in his face
        To cause him blindness, too!

The LEADING FIGURE *waves the cross before the face of* PARACELSUS, *who stares at him a moment, as if contemplating some reply, then thinks better of it, and with a derisive shrug moves away with* FRANZ. *They take a circuitous route to the top level of the set, returning to where the hooded figures have shunned hoods to become townspeople — inn keeper, tailor, merchant, priest.*

As PARACELSUS *and* FRANZ *leave, the hooded* FIGURES *smash the laboratory, and, in mime, exorcise the rubble with the cross.*

FRANZ: The church is in uproar — their terror
     Now precedes us.

PARACELSUS: Their church can go to hell for all I care!
     Their hypocrisy and cant has stripped them
     Of all claims to dignity . . .
     Their buildings and cathedrals
     Are nothing more than barns now
     Occupied by fat and lazy herders . . .
     Their sermons and manners are but imitations
     Of posturing magicians . . .
     Speak no more of Church and God
     In the same breath —
     For it demeans and humiliates
     The God I know and love!

They approach the townspeople, who watch them sternly.

FRANZ: Gentlemen — we have been on foot since sunrise,
     With neither food nor drink. . . .
     My master and I are weary,
     And desire food and lodging,
     At reasonable cost,
     For we have little more than travel money.

INN KEEPER *glances at the* PRIEST, *who nods, and turns away.*

INN KEEPER: Is this man Paracelsus, the famed healer?

FRANZ: That he is, and I am Franz,
     His servant and apprentice.

The INN KEEPER *shakes his head.*

INN KEEPER: I would it were different or another evening.
     But peddlars, merchants and soldiers
     Now fully occupy my lodgings.

FRANZ: Is there a porch then . . . a barn,
    Or some abandoned shop where we might. . . .

PARACELSUS: Do not beg, lad . . . observe the priest —
    His face shrieks in its silence
    As the page of a forbidden book!

PRIEST *(Stammering)*:
    Ho . . . how dare you, heathen?

INN KEEPER *(Nervously)*:

    I do not lie to you, Paracelsus!
    Had I the wherewithal, I would be most happy
    To have your famed person as guest
    Within my inn!

PARACELSUS *(Angry now)*:
    You *do* lie, and may God spare you
    The punishment you deserve for your unmanliness!
    What has become of our German race of men
    Who now cower like slavish dogs
    Before the cowled hooligans of Rome?

The PRIEST *spins on his heel and strikes* PARACELSUS *across the face with his hand.* PARACELSUS *staggers back, then regains his balance. He stares at the priest.*

PARACELSUS *(Coldly)*:
    Weary with hunger and fatigue, for I have travelled
    Many miles this day, doctoring the stricken
    I come by night upon this town . . .
    To be struck across the face by you —
    Wanton scum unfit to dust my shoes . . .
    What is your proper German name?
    So if I should chance to meet your mother
    In my wanderings, I may share with her
    The grief she bears at giving birth to you!

More out of panic than anger now, the PRIEST *strikes* PARACELSUS *again.* FRANZ *tries to defend him, but is pushed aside by another* TOWNSMAN. PARACELSUS *is knocked down.*

INN KEEPER: If you've hurt him,
    God in Heaven will not forgive us!

The PRIEST, *in his own fear, becomes excitable.*

PRIEST: No! God rejoices in this act — believe me!
       Feel free to fall upon him now!
       The doctor you respected is no more . . .
       He has sold his talents to the devil —
       So fall upon him! God will forgive you!

But the PRIEST *cannot entice the others to attack. They are awed by the prostrate body before them, and retreat, followed by the* PRIEST.

DR. WEBB *and* DR. GUZA *stroll back and forth on lowest level of set, as if pacing up and down a hospital hallway.*

DR. GUZA *(Shaking her head)*: You're a gentle person, and yet if I didn't know you . . . .

DR. WEBB: Lay off me, will you! . . . That's your husband's bag, if he's studying for the ministry!

DR. GUZA: You should meet him — how about dinner at our house next week?

DR. WEBB: Betty, I like women, but I don't get along with men worth a damn! *Smiles.* Especially the ones committed to save the world.

DR. GUZA: Keep talking like that an' you'll end up believing what you say.

DR. WEBB: I want to be left alone, Betty.

He is tense, no longer smiling.

DR. GUZA: Why?

DR. WEBB: Because I can *pretend* to be human, and not have to live the part. Can you understand that?

DR. GUZA: No.

DR. WEBB *laughs.*

CURTAIN

ACT III

Curtain up.

PARACELSUS, *ragged and dirty, and followed by* FRANZ, *crosses top eleva-*
tion of set. FRANZ *is breathless, and pauses for rest.*

Sound of dogs in background, yelping angrily in pursuit.

A peasant MAN *and* WOMAN *enter. The man is limping badly, and leaning*
on the woman. PARACELSUS *sees them, and wordlessly goes to them. Kneel-*
ing before the man and lifting his pantleg, PARACELSUS *exposes a badly cut*
and discoloured leg. Unscrewing the hasp of his sword, he withdraws tinc-
tures and salves, which he applies to the wound. Then from his satchel he
takes dressings, with which he covers the wound. The peasant MAN *and*
WOMAN *bow to him and leave, their heads low.*

Still on his knees, he receives a procession of other people who enter, all
ragged, all silent, averting his gaze. He treats, examines and comforts them.

FRANZ: We slept in fields. . . . For food I stole
      Vegetables from gardens and the marketplace. . . .
      I lay awake at night, listening to his frail body
      Rasp for breath . . . and always, the pursuing dogs
      Barking and yowling near at hand, on command
      Of the henchmen of the church — the mystic brotherhoods,
      And community of doctors throughout Germany and
      Switzerland.

The last patient is treated and leaves. PARACELSUS *stares for a long mo-*
ment at FRANZ, *who sits with his head in his hands, ashamed of his weariness*
and despair.

DR. WEBB *and* DR. GUZA *enter on lowest level of stage. They are dressed*
in tennis clothes, and carry racquets. They watch an invisible game off-stage
as they await their turn on the courts.

DR. GUZA: It's a good farm . . . a place where children can ride
  horses on holidays. . . .

DR. WEBB: How much did it cost?

DR. GUZA: Thirty thousand. . . .

DR. WEBB: You're wasting your money. Thirty thousand in industrial
  stock is better investment than some rundown old farm!

DR. GUZA: It's worth forty now!

88

DR. WEBB: Which is no more than inflationary loss on the money you've invested. I can tell you of ways to beat the system, if you're interested.

DR. GUZA (*Annoyed*): Why is it that everything is an absolute value with you? When we invest, it's not because we plan to make more money . . . we don't need it!

DR. WEBB: On this continent, honey, commerce is like sex — essential and guilt-ridden!

DR. GUZA: You're a fascist!

DR. WEBB: You know why I dislike small "L" liberals?

DR. GUZA (*Sarcastically*): Do tell me, so I, too, may see the light!

DR. WEBB: They're all self-righteous bastards, trying to keep a foot in each world! You can't have it both ways — either you oppress, or you're oppressed! Either you manipulate food, or you'll end up being the hungry one! . . . There's not enough to go around . . . that's the short and long of it, Betty! Something has to die for other things to live!

DR. GUZA *stares angrily at him.*

DR. GUZA: What sort of doctor are you?

DR. WEBB: I'm not smug and outside this world, if that's what you mean. *With anguish.* Look, honey . . . I'm lookin' for the answers too! I'm reacting out of self-preservation . . . if someone has the answer, I wish they'd tell me! There's got to be room for those of us who've become hard-eyed conservatives . . . I'm a good doctor . . . you said so yourself.

DR. GUZA *walks quickly past him.*

DR. GUZA: Come on. . . . There's a couple leaving!

He follows her. They exit.

PARACELSUS: I can endure for entirity . . .
        But it is wrong of me to torture
        Your young body and your mind
        In pursuit of things known only to my enemies,
        For my friends have left me now.

FRANZ *rises hurriedly to his feet and joins* PARACELSUS. *They continue walking, making their way to another elevation, where a fat, haughty* BURGOMASTER *is carefully packing a clay pipe for smoking.*

FRANZ: It is nothing . . . sleep will help me.

PARACELSUS *(To Burgomaster, in a pleading tone)*:
    Is this Innsbruck, brother?

BURGOMASTER: It is, and your brother I am not!
    Who are you? What is the nature
    Of your business at this hour of evening?

PARACELSUS: I am Paracelsus, the healer,
    And I request permission to practice
    In this town!

The BURGOMASTER *lights his pipe slowly, blows smoke into the face of* PARACELSUS, *then smiles coldly.*

BURGOMASTER: You — are Paracelsus? . . . Begone!
    I know the great Paracelsus as I know this hand!
    I'll set my dogs upon you for your impertinence, beggar!
    Take you and this ruffian lad, and be gone!
    Paracelsus, indeed. . . .

PARACELSUS *chokes back his anger.*

PARACELSUS: I will not beg . . . I cannot beg.
    I am a doctor and request permission
    To pursue my skills. . . .
    If I am not Paracelsus whom you know
    Better, it appears, than I know him—
    Then let me practice as a doctor—
    Any doctor . . . nameless, if you wish!

BURGOMASTER *(Sarcastically)*:
    Might I ask to examine
    Your degree . . .*Doctor*?

PARACELSUS: I have no degrees, but leave me an hour
    With ten of your most ill citizens
    And my competence will not be questioned.

BURGOMASTER: Don't play the fool with me, you impertinent bastard!
    A man in rags is not a doctor. . . .
    You are a swineherd, perhaps,
    Or at worst, a beggar! Stand aside!
    I have an evening meal waiting for me.

PARACELSUS: Damn you and all those like you,
    Who created only doctors clad in silk,

And not in shabby rags grilled by the sun . . .
What a mockery you've made
Of practitioners of healing!

The BURGOMASTER *spits at the feet of* PARACELSUS *and walks past him to exit.* PARACELSUS *unscrews hilt of his sword and gives* FRANZ *a leather pouch.*

PARACELSUS: Take this laudanum, Franz. . . .
Be sparing with the scalpel,
But when you must cut flesh or bone
Be merciful and generous in turning
Deepest pain to sleep. . . .

FRANZ *takes the drug pouch and watches* PARACELSUS *uncertainly.*

FRANZ: Are we to go . . . in separate directions now?

PARACELSUS: From here on, I know not where
My destiny will take me.
I have premonitions of an early death . . .
You must go your way and fulfill
Work destined for a younger man.

FRANZ *(Shocked)*:
I wish to stay — to share
Whatever fate befalls you!

PARACELSUS: It is the fate of man to struggle
Against nature and his baser self.
His ultimate salvation is in loneliness.
I no longer ask — I command you leave!
You are a good lad and a competent physician.
May God be gentler to you
Than I have been. . . .

He turns abruptly. Distant sound of barking dogs. PARACELSUS *points and snarls.*

PARACELSUS: Hear that? We, who make sport for the gods,
Are hunted to the end!

PARACELSUS *exits.* FRANZ *moves slowly to highest levels of set.*

FRANZ: The miles separating us
Became years. . . .

Procession of people begin to pass below FRANZ.

FRANZ (*Calling to procession*): What news?

WOMAN: The plague is nearing Stertzing!

FRANZ: Are there doctors in the town?

WOMAN: No—they've left. But Paracelsus
Is arriving!

FRANZ: How fares the old man?

ANOTHER WOMAN: He is bookish and ill-tempered,
Never sleeping—harsh as frost;
But as a healer—
God Himself could not do more!

FRANZ *laughs.*

FRANZ: Affliction and misery has met its match
In the homeopathy of his being!

WOMAN: Nothing is eternal—particularly
The wisdom of a noble man. . . .
Paracelsus will in time die
And we shall once again be tortured
With illness . . . and its cures!

FRANZ *waves cheerfully to the procession. They wave back, laughing, and exit.*

FRANZ: For the longest time, I heard nothing
From him—and then one night,
I was awaked from my sleep,
As if shaken by a nurse . . .
And when I woke, I heard
Within my brain his voice. . . .

PARACELSUS (*Off stage*):
Franz — do you hear me?
Have I communion with you?

FRANZ: Yes, Theophrastus!
But you are not with me!

PARACELSUS (*Off stage*):
I am well and occupied productively. . . .
I have lately studied the transfer of thoughts
Over distances so vast that no phenomena
Of voice or presence can equate this feat!

FRANZ: Your thoughts reach me as if
You were present in this very room!

PARACELSUS (*Entering on level below Franz, books in his hands*):
I cannot write you as I know not
Where you are. But I have
Some observations to provide you. . . .
Diseases of the mind are not the work
Of forces emanating from the devil —
They are natural diseases as all others;
Treat them accordingly. . . . I have found
Conclusive evidence of an unseen astral body
Within man — as in plants, capable of instant
Flight to distant places. Also,
I have found much that is curious and useful
In the arts of clairvoyance and levitation —
Do not neglect further studies of these things.
I have much to tell you of amulets,
To counter influences of forces electric
Which affect the human spirit and the body . . . .

FRANZ, *turned away from* PARACELSUS, *is writing furiously.*

FRANZ: I make note of your instructions!

PARACELSUS: Believe in God and love,
But not the God or love which bears
Official approval, lad —
For every fool praises his own club!
He who stands on the Pope
Stands on a cushion! . . .
He who stands on Zwingli
Stands on emptiness! . . .
He who stands on Luther,
Stands on a waterpipe! *Laughs.*
Remain true to your inner wisdom,
The finest mind is an empty vessel
At the time of birth — fill it!

FRANZ *also laughs, nods, and puts away his notes.*

PARACELSUS *seats himself on a small wooden bench and opens his books.
He takes out a small piece of cheese from his pocket and munches thoughtfully
on it.*

FRANZ: . . . Nine months later, I did hear from him —
        A messenger brought me news and a summons
        To leave at once for Salzburg,
        For Paracelsus feared that he was dying.
        I turned my practice over to a trusted colleague
        And filled with apprehension, journeyed to that city . . .

FRANZ *exits quickly.*

PARACELSUS: I have this day learned of the death
        Of my father, whom I had wished to visit,
        But my travels now are slow and tortured . . . .

His hands tremble and the lump of cheese falls to his feet. He suddenly becomes very old and frail.

PARACELSUS: Farewell, gentle parent — may your deserved rest
        Not be marred by pain and holocaust
        The living share. . . . I have lately dreamed
        In short moments of my sleep, of my infancy . . .
        Of my mother, poor demented soul — holding me to her. . . .

He holds his arms in a crook before him, as a mother comforting an infant.

PARACELSUS: Her fearful eyes, dark as the forests
        Of the Edsel . . . her lips mute
        On her suffering . . . Oh, God!
        Had I the time left to repay her love
        For me with further studies
        On congenital insanity!

Sound of the bells of Einsedeln.

On topmost level of set, WOMAN-ANGEL *appears, hooded and dressed in black.*

On the level of Paracelsus, three hooded, mystic FIGURES *armed with cudgels enter silently.* PARACELSUS *looks at each of them, an expression of profound sadness on his face.*

LEADER OF GROUP: It took us many years to find the place
        And the moment for this meeting, Paracelsus!
        Your screams will not be heard —
        The streets are empty now . . .
        The stairway and the entrance to this house
        Has been deserted of your patients
        And ragged students and admirers!

94

PARACELSUS *peers at the leader of the group.*

PARACELSUS: Is it you, Oporinus?

On his words, a youthful STUDENT *enters, hat in hand. He is well-dressed, bedecked with jewellery. Throughout following conversation,* PARACELSUS *peers into hooded face of leader of the group.*

The student in memory is OPORINUS.

OPORINUS: My good wishes for your health,
      Dear teacher, and master
      Of all physicians!

PARACELSUS: What is it, Oporinus? Your wishes
      For my health heralds a request for money
      Or approaching fear of death . . .
      You seem hearty!

OPORINUS *(Grinning)*:
      You jest, do you not, sir?

PARACELSUS: I know you better than our Lord
      Knew Judas — what is it now?

OPORINUS: I was a dedicated student of yours,
      Was I not?

PARACELSUS: No, you were not!

The smile fades from the STUDENT'S *face.*

OPORINUS: Why do you punish me with rudeness —
      Yet keep as confidant and friend
      That pale peasant, Franz?

PARACELSUS *(Sighs)*: You bore me with your treachery.
      You know well why I dismissed you, Oporinus —
      Consider it your fortune I had much to do,
      Which spared you the thrashing you deserved —
      You knave that dogs my heels as a gaunt crow
      A gasping sheep!

OPORINUS: I was paid . . . you know by whom . . .
      To write that public letter as a student,
      Denouncing you as drunkard
      On your journey to your friends
      In Zurich . . . It was my wife;
      You know that wife of mine,

Who desires finery and a house
Beyond the limit of my earnings . . .
Forgive my weakness —
But I am a driven man,
Having married foolishly. . . .

PARACELSUS: She deserves you, Oporinus — and you, her!
Never grieve — you are a knave and fool,
But still you are no worse than others
I have trained through apprenticeship and lectures
Doctors in the hundreds — yet other than Franz
Whom you resent, of true healers
I have trained so few . . .
Two from Pannonia — three from Poland;
One from Bohemia, and one from Holland.
So much energy, for such a scant reward!
What is it you have come to beg this time?

OPORINUS: I . . . do sorely need . . . some precious laudanum.
I have three patients of great wealth
Who would see me through the darkest times
Of my debts if I but had a small container
Of the drug . . . Paracelsus, please!
I am otherwise a ruined man!

With pained fingers, PARACELSUS *fumbles in his pockets, and taking out
a small package, throws it over his shoulder.* OPORINUS *falls to the floor
to eagerly collect it.*

PARACELSUS: Here, you worthless bastard!
May this give your wealthy patients
Needed sleep from the ravages
Of alcohol and whoring!

OPORINUS: Thank you, good friend and teacher!
I will repay you when I can,
I promise you!

PARACELSUS: Yes, you will repay me . . .
When might I expect to read another
Infamy above your signature?
Accusing me of what this time?
Black magic? Monsters?
A servant of the devil?

OPORINUS *flees and exits.*

PARACELSUS (*To Leader of Group*):
> Are you in the pay of priests and doctors?
> . . . Or is your hatred such
> That a century of waiting
> Would not have cooled it
> One degree?

LEADER OF GROUP: That is a question you may ponder for eternity.
> May your master, the devil, take pity
> On your revolutionary soul!
> There will be none on earth . . .
> So long as earth endures!

The WOMAN-ANGEL *signals. The three hooded* MEN *attack* PARACELSUS *in slow motion, in a scene of cruel medieval assassination.*

PARACELSUS *gives a low, moaning outcry as he lifts his arthritic, twisted hands to defend himself. But he is helpless over the blows of the clubs against the back of his head. He falls.*

DR. WEBB *and* DR. GUZA *enter, still in tennis wear. They have just concluded their game. They are in animated argument.*

DR. WEBB: Alright — then forget it! I don't worry about me . . . but you do!

DR. GUZA: You're totally out of it, you know that?

DR. WEBB: Do I steal? Break up homes? Abuse my patients? . . . What is it?

DR. GUZA: No . . . no! What you represent is far worse than that! You would, in the last crunch, stand in the way of progress!

DR. WEBB: Sure I would, so would you. So would your preacher-husband . . . only I admit I would! But what is progress? Giving every fool the right to vote himself a car for a faster ride to hell? Providing antibiotics to populations who will die of hunger?

DR. GUZA: There is always hope for new ideas. . . . That's the value of mistakes . . . that's what great men are all about!

DR. WEBB: You can take your great men and put them down the tube, for all I care. They generally don't live long enough to see the harm they've done. The most this world can take with a minimum of damage is *competent* people. Great people scare me . . . they scare all of us.

DR. GUZA: What sort of damned nonsense is that?

DR. WEBB: We all voted for stringing Christ up on the cross — that's why we survived to make children, study medicine, create hybrid corn and fan-jet engines! And we'll do it again, and again . . . and again. There's nothing wrong with that — it's even democratic, because there are always more of us than you! Relax, honey — the kid you lost on the ward yesterday was just an average human being!

DR. GUZA *turns away from him and begins to sob.*

DR. WEBB *(Soberly)*: What choices have we got? . . . What choices has anybody? I don't believe in God or people . . . I believe in myself being capable of doing good things sometimes—and even that seems difficult to accomplish.

DR. GUZA *leaves him. He watches her exit. Bunting a tennis ball thoughtfully with his racquet, he exits in the opposite direction.*

The slow motion assassination of PARACELSUS *goes on. He is caked with blood, but still rises to his knees to escape, protecting the back of his head with his hands.*

ANOTHER MEMBER OF GROUP *(Turning away, making a retching sound)*:
     He won't die! . . . His skull is smashed and he
     Won't die!

The WOMAN-ANGEL *makes a frantic signal. The* KILLERS *lower their clubs. The* LEADER *of the group props* PARACELSUS *up against the bench. The* KILLERS *hurry away.* WOMAN-ANGEL *remains motionless on top level of set, looking down on* PARACELSUS.

Bells of Einsedeln peal loudly, then recede into background.

PARACELSUS *shudders. His speech is halting and painful.*

PARACELSUS: Though I have lived through the agony
          Of this moment once before,
          I have forgotten the excruciating pain . . .
          The helions of light that dance
          Before my eyes . . . the growing chill
          That deepens through my flesh . . .
          All feeling now has left my arms and legs . . . .

          . . . Left for dead, I did not die . . .
          But raised by face from the acid,
          Thickening blood to cry for help. . . .
          A drunken mason, passing by, did hear me . . .

>Helped raise me to my bed and took my message
>To what friends I still possessed. . . .
>The rest is but a matter of an hour
>Or a day, before the vital organs
>Surrender in despair to the skull,
>Shattered in a hundred pieces . . . .

He raises his hand past his open eyes.

PARACELSUS: . . . Now the hallucinations come . . .
>Like visions of a prior life . . .
>How melancholy I do feel . . . Father?
>Is that you? . . . Some nights I saw you
>In my inner eye, hunched alone —
>Your mouth drawn with age and sadness . . .
>Sitting at a solitary table to a meal
>You could not eat — your wife dead . . .
>Your son a frightening legend . . .
>And you, old man, dreaming of a life
>Of companions, children and domestic love . . .
>Until the spittle in your throat dried
>To bitter ashes of regret. . . .

A distraught young WOMAN *enters, carrying a dead child.* PARACELSUS *blinks and half rises, reaching out to her.*

WOMAN: Paracelsus — healer from the gods!
>My child is dead!
>And so is his father —
>Killed in their wretched wars!

PARACELSUS: God, oh God! . . . Why do people suffer so?

WOMAN *(Handing dead child to Paracelsus):*
>Make him live! Please make him live!

PARACELSUS: I cannot help you — I, too, am dead!
>Let sorrow for us both well from your heart
>Like some gigantic storm, threatening screams
>To wake Him who created us for grief . . .
>Rend your clothes and skin . . . plunge headlong
>Into flames of suicide or depravity . . .
>Cry to the heavens if it helps . . .
>Cry for both of us!

WOMAN *(Screaming)*:
>Help us all, doctor!
>You cannot die now!

PARACELSUS: The love I bore for you surpassed children . . .
>Parents . . . husbands . . . lovers . . .
>All, except the love of God Himself
>For man and woman. . . .

He cradles the dead child with great tenderness and compassion. The WOMAN
weeps quietly now, and removing her shawl, covers PARACELSUS *with it.*
Then tearing off a strip of cloth from her skirt, she wipes his face.

PARACELSUS: He suffered much . . . it is written in the purple flashes
>In his face . . . frightened, too young to understand
>The philosophy of punishments for which
>There was no crime . . . . *Looks up at Woman.*
>You are mother to twenty children yet unborn . . .
>Builders of houses and roads as yet unplanned . . .
>Nurses . . . caretakers of the fields . . .
>Rowdies and lovers . . . Some in splendid health . . .
>Some maimed—but your own!
>Bury what is dead, and turn to life again . . . .
>Healers will attend you, and God,
>Through His meadowlarks and nightingales
>Will sing His celebration for your homecoming
>From the deep, dark abyss that confronts us all . . . .

The WOMAN *nods, takes the dead child, and pressing the hand of*
PARACELSUS *to her cheek, leaves.*

PARACELSUS *(Shouting)*:
>Men of strong heart!
>Who swore to walk erect into the raging storms . . .
>Where are you now? . . . What jest of gods
>Hobbles you — Women? Luxury? Fear?
>Paracelsus calls you for the final time!

The bells of Einsedeln go silent.

Sounds of crickets. Distant barking of dogs.

FRANZ, *well-dressed and prosperous, enters. He is followed by six*
WITNESSES.

On entering, FRANZ *stops some distance from* PARACELSUS, *and motions*
to others to do likewise.

FRANZ: When your message reached me, I came
As quickly as I could . . . travelling
By night and day . . . stopping only
To change horses ridden at full gallop. . . .

PARACELSUS: I care not if you flew or galloped . . .
Only that you've arrived in time, Franz.
Smiles at him. You've fleshed out . . .
Your hair has paled . . . I asked you
To bring six witnesses to hear
My testament. . . .

FRANZ: They are here . . . .

He turns his face away from PARACELSUS.

FRANZ: You are in hemorrhage, Theophrastus!
The years of work with antimony, mercury,
Opium, nightshade, monkshood and other poisons
In distillation near your body now rise in revenge!
. . . I cannot bear the pain within your eyes . . .
The hollow cheeks and thin lips of an ancient man . . .
Theophrastus — you are only ten years older than myself!

PARACELSUS: Your diagnosis is a hasty one, Franz . . .
Whatever ravages the skills of my profession
Wreak within my flesh and bones is nothing
To what men have done with clubs to the hindmost
Portions of my head. . . .

Leans forward painfully.

PARACELSUS: I tried to live until I saw you . . . .

FRANZ *hurries to him, bends down to examine the back of* PARACELSUS' *head,
then turns away, his face registering horror.*

FRANZ: Who has done this to him — why? . . .
The entire skull in back is crushed
And hanging by some strips of scalp. . . .
The brain, white and swollen,
Is exposed and drying. . . .

FRANZ *(To Paracelsus)*: I will gather the finest doctors in this city
And we will tend you to good health!

PARACELSUS: No, Franz. . . . Let God and I agree
Upon the moment of my death —

Each man has that right, and neither
Doctor, priest, magician or the king himself
Should interfere when the injuries are hopeless!

FRANZ *paces with fury.*

FRANZ: What villain did this to you?
I will revenge your death!

PARACELSUS *(Weary)*:
Only old enemies avenge old slights . . .
Say it was some doctors, magicians and the priests . . .
I know their names, but will not reveal them . . .
What hour is it, Franz?

FRANZ: It is evening now.

PARACELSUS: By night . . . thieves steal when they cannot be seen . . .
So creeps in death when medicine is at its darkest
And steals away the life of man —
His greatest treasure.

FRANZ *motions for the* WITNESSES *to come forward. They are nervous and respectful. One of them takes out paper and sits. The moment* PARACELSUS *speaks, he begins to write.*

PARACELSUS: Write this then. . . .

Bells of Einsedeln begin to ring.

The three ASSASSINS *enter. The* WOMAN-ANGEL *comes down to hover near* PARACELSUS. *The three* ASSASSINS *again mime the killing of* PARACELSUS *in slow motion. They are invisible to witnesses and* FRANZ. *Each time he is struck,* PARACELSUS *lurches and struggles with the agony. But he no longer lifts his hands to defend himself against the blows.*

PARACELSUS: . . . I, Theophrastus von Hohenheim . . . clear in mind
. . . And of upright heart . . . commit my life,
Death and soul to the care and protection
Of Almighty God . . . In the steadfast hope
That the Merciful God will not allow
The bitter suffering, martyrdom and death
Of His only Son . . . our saviour Jesus Christ . . .
To be fruitless and of no avail to him,
A miserable man. . . .

PARACELSUS *lurches from a blow. One of the witnesses presses a flask of water to his lips, but the liquid runs helplessly down his chin. He gazes at the man with gratitude, and shrugs to indicate it cannot be helped.*

FRANZ: What barbaric villainy drives men
          To inflict such injury on men among us,
          Who in their deeds, wisdom and compassion
          Surpass the God we claim to love above all else?
          I am not a violent man, but I could sack a city
          For this act!

PARACELSUS: I died . . . once . . . long ago . . .
          But interpreters through passing ages . . .
          Do this to me . . . for their own discoveries . . .
          Of hope . . . futility . . . and perchance some glimmer
          Of eternal reason . . . why man is cursed
          With choices in the way he lives and dies . . . .

FRANZ: I beg you — condemn them all by name!

PARACELSUS: Death is not fearsome, my beloved Franz . . .
          Nor angry . . . be not afraid for me . . .
          It is my days' work ended . . .
          And God's harvest time . . .
          Man's power over us — ends with death.
          Only God deals with us then,
          And God is love!

Another blow, which throws him forward. An uncertainty flashes over his face.

PARACELSUS: God *must* be love!
          Else why this turbulent intelligence
          And rage to serve the species
          To exclusion of all else? Why?

FRANZ *cautions him to rest. But another blow rocks him.*

FRANZ: I beg you — rest a moment!
          The cavern in your skull
          Has begun to bleed afresh
          With your efforts!

PARACELSUS, *with a mighty effort, flings his covers to the floor and staggers to his feet to confront his* KILLERS, *who move back in slow motion.* ·

PARACELSUS: I am aflame! No glaciers nor oceans
       Can quell my fevers now! . . . Bury you my body
       . . . Among the poor beyond the bridge . . .
       At the church of St. Sebastian . . .
       Between the singing of the psalms,
       Give you a penny each to every poor man and woman
       Assembled for my funeral
       . . . My father haunts me like a winter's night! . . .
       I did not know . . . the day he died . . .
       So many years ago. . . . Had he called for me,
       His son? . . . And I, deaf to his pleas . . . .

FRANZ (*Desperately lying*):
       Be assured he died in peace . . . my sister
       Was a servant in his house . . .
       He died in peace, she told me!

PARACELSUS: Thank God for that!

He continues standing, gazing on his circling KILLERS *and the* WOMAN-
ANGEL *who directs them.*

PARACELSUS: Pay my debts, Franz. . . . Assemble all my books . . .
       From wherever I have left them . . .
       My complements of drugs and tinctures
       And have Doctor Wendle in this city
       . . . Care for them . . . so long as life
       Is with him — he is a scholar and a careful man.
       Pay yourselves twelve gulden each . . .
       For your troubles here this night . . .
       Disperse the rest to all my heirs . . .
       The poor, miserable, needy people . . .
       Without favour or disfavour. . . .
       Poverty and want are the only qualifications . . .
       To you, beloved Franz . . . I bequeath my sword
       And this amulet about my throat . . . .

Hands it to FRANZ.

PARACELSUS: . . . And the most fearful legacy of all . . .
       The curse of continual enquiry . . .
       Plus my eternal love to lift you to the lip
       Of heaven, while still you pace and prod
       This earth for what truth and honesty
       Still unknown lies buried in the herbs,

Stones and essences like a mantel of the gods . . .
Waiting to redress human pain and want . . . .

With a groan, PARACELSUS *topples and falls. The stage darkens as a procession of people with candles in their hands enter and weave their way through the upper two elevations.* WOMAN-ANGEL, ASSASSINS *and* PARACELSUS *disappear into and become part of, the moving bodies. A flame flickers back of set and continues burning, throwing entire set outline into silhouette. Candles multiply. Darkened set becomes gloomier with more moving bodies.*

FRANZ *moves forward for final address to audience.*

FRANZ: Paracelsus . . . healer, philosopher, teacher
And stormy petrel of medical renaissance . . .
Died and was buried on the twenty-fourth day
Of September, 1541 . . . St. Rupert's festival day.
Through the next day and into the night,
The poor thronged the city,
As if knowing through some revelation
Of his passing. . . .

Momentary burst of human voices.

FRANZ: Thousands came . . . thousands unto thousands . . .
Filled the streets, and still they came . . .
Not knowing where or how he died . . .
Only that he had come to rest in Salzburg . . . .
Thousands and still more thousands . . .
Moving slowly through the streets,
Carrying tapers which they lit at twilight . . .
As if in honour of the greatest saint . . .
Thousands upon thousands . . . The tapers lit
Until at midnight the city was a slowly
Moving sheet of living flame . . .
Orders were dispatched to silence
All the city bells, lest they excite
Some violence against the murderers
And those of wealth and privilege
Who could scarce disguise their pleasure
At his death. . . .

Babble of voices ends suddenly.

FRANZ: But at midnight, as if on signal,
The moving river of the country's people stopped. . . .

Candelight procession of people stop.

FRANZ: And a great silence settled over them . . .
　　　　More frightening than a howl of pain . . .
　　　　And then . . . With a sigh as soft as summer wind . . .
　　　　The candles which they held were all blown out. . . .

Candles in procession are blown out in unison. Outline light of flame continues.

FRANZ: And in the darkness . . . the tallow-incense
　　　　Burned like acid in the nose. . . .

Bells of Einsedeln begin to peal loudly.

SLOW CURTAIN.

Prometheus Bound

108

Dramatis Personae

PROMETHEUS	A man.
POWER	Security agent. A man.
FORCE	Security agent. A woman.
HEPHAESTUS	Security director. A man.
OCEANUS	Admiral of the navy. A man.
FARMER	A man.
WORKER	A man.
IO	A woman.
HERMES	Courier and expediter. A man.
ARGUS	A dead man.

(Notes: Re: music and songs. — The melody of IO'S SONG establishes the precise beat for the drum sounds. To establish this, four or eight drum beats should be used between verses of the song at the top of the play. That beat then occurs where drums are indicated. Music of IO'S SONG is to be played on clarinet or flute where music in background is indicated. SONG OF PROMETHEUS would be better sung unaccompanied, if possible.)

Drum beats in darkness.

IO'S SONG

I walk the burning streets
A lantern in my hand
And no one knows me . . .

Ten thousand hooded men
Have memorized my face
Yet look beyond me . . .

I board the screaming jets
And walk through tunnelled earth
A lonely stranger . . .

Now that Prometheus is bound
There's no freedom to be found
Except in danger . . .

Poor Prometheus is bound
There's no freedom to be found
Except in danger . . . .

Lights up slowly. Drum beats continue.

Light up on a set which consists of two sleeping ramps rising to point in back centre stage. This suggests an emotional infinity.

Playing areas are on the ramps and in front of set. A third playing area is the nether world below the point where the ramps meet back stage centre.

The set should suggest an abandoned cavern under the earth where some military or isolated technological facility had once functioned, but has since been stripped away leaving torn piping, gathering moisture and decay, burning gas fires from poorly sealed cut pipes, etc. An enormous tomb for debris and dead things of the world above.

Enter POWER *and* FORCE *with a chained and gagged* PROMETHEUS *between them.* PROMETHEUS *is dishevelled and showing signs of fatigue and much physical punishment. They handle* PROMETHEUS *roughly as they escort and force him to the position of his final incarceration. They then kick the feet out from under* PROMETHEUS *in a graceful and cruel choreography and turn to wait at attention for* HEPHAESTUS, *who stumbles up to them. He is breathless and fearful.*
Drum beat sounds heighten then die abruptly.

POWER: This is it.

FORCE *(Rapidly):* We've done it!

POWER: No interference — not a sign of protest from the people . . . .

FORCE: No fanfare or debate in the press or on television . . . .

POWER: The Deputy was captured, sentenced and delivered here in the back of a sanitation truck . . . .

FORCE: He's come down a bit . . . .

POWER: That he has . . . how much smaller he seems now.

FORCE: No more rides through the cities in open state cars. No more speeches to the people or debates in government to confuse every issue.

HEPHAESTUS: Enough! You've done your work well. I'll see you're commended to the ministry.

POWER: Shall we prepare the usual report on how the prisoner was found . . . that he resisted?

HEPHAESTUS: I'll look after the paperwork. Our mission is not yet completed.

POWER: No problem with that. Now that we've got him here and no one the wiser for it, the last chore is just technical.

*(*FORCE *is suddenly agitated.)*

FORCE: He betrayed our homeland — sold military and security secrets — yet he lives.

HEPHAESTUS *(Sharply):* That was the decision of the tribunal. It has nothing to do with us!

FORCE: A confessed traitor deserves to die!

HEPHAESTUS (More sharply): He confessed to nothing. The tribunal verdict is all we are assigned to execute — nothing less and nothing more!

FORCE: If he'd been shot trying to escape . . . or trapped here by some explosion, I know our First Minister would be much happier than —

HEPHAESTUS: One more word, lieutenant, and I'll have you cited for insubordination!

(She snaps to attention.)

FORCE: I'm sorry, sir!

HEPHAESTUS (Wearily): I would've given ten years of my life to be a thousand miles from this place today . . . .

POWER: Are you well . . . is something wrong, sir?

HEPHAESTUS: I can't release you from your manacles Prometheus — never again . . . . But can we get you some water?

FORCE: Sir . . . the regulations forbid . . . .

HEPHAESTUS: Damn what the regulations say! The man is dying! (Stares at each of them) For how long, and how many of you did it take to do this before he was brought to me?

FORCE: He . . . resisted, sir.

(HEPHAESTUS laughs bitterly and shakes his head.)

HEPHAESTUS: As the hundreds of others over the past twenty years resisted!

POWER: Sir?

HEPHAESTUS: I have seen men with broken skulls brought before the tribunal and asked to recite confessions of treason and betrayal. Most would have difficulty remembering their names . . . . (Motioning to PROMETHEUS) He knew. He even sanctioned many arrests and convictions of those who questioned the direction of our affairs . . . . How badly hurt do you think he is?

(POWER turns away, uncertain of his answer.)

POWER: He . . . might as well be dead.

HEPHAESTUS: Because of injuries sustained? Or injuries to come?

POWER: Both, sir.

HEPHAESTUS: Let him rest a moment before he is administered the final tender mercies of our judicial process.

POWER: As you wish, sir.

(HEPHAESTUS *moves away and* POWER *and* FORCE *follow.*)

HEPHAESTUS: He and I . . . we were both elected deputies by the people in our region. Did you know that?

POWER: No, sir. I didn't.

HEPHAESTUS: We were deputies from the same region, but beyond that, we had few similarities. He was returned time and again as a deputy, while I found and accepted work in the civil service. What a man he was! *(Laughs)* Thoughts came to him like that! *(Snaps his fingers)* No matter how complex the problem, he saw resolutions days before they occurred to others. But when he lost his temper — get out of the way and hide! Never saw a man could get that angry . . . .

POWER: Excuse me, sir. But . . . are you afraid to do what must be done?

(HEPHAESTUS *turns and stares at him, his face saddened.*)

HEPHAESTUS: No. After all these years in the security service I have learned not to be afraid . . . only cautious.

FORCE: I don't understand. Tell us what's to be done and we'll do it. Gladly, knowing that what we do is . . . .

HEPHAESTUS: Never be glad of anything you must do! Do it with as little passion as you would if you were adjusting a troublesome machine. Or preparing food for a picnic. The winds of our country change from time to time . . . and when they do, those with passion this morning become victims of their passion by nightfall. Remember that, if you wish to live a long life.

POWER: You make decisions you must feel strongly about.

HEPHAESTUS: My decisions are forced on me, young man.

POWER: By our superiors — the ministry?

HEPHAESTUS: By our beloved First Minister. And others like him. A God without disciples would be a nobody.

FORCE: I don't like hearing such talk . . . .

HEPHAESTUS *(Unhappily):* That seems to be the majority sentiment of our times.

(Turns to PROMETHEUS.)

HEPHAESTUS: He was not like that.

FORCE: I'll say he wasn't. A confessed traitor.

HEPHAESTUS: Let us say there were two faces to Prometheus. What we have brought here is the condemned political leader.

FORCE: That is all there is, sir.

HEPHAESTUS: Oh, no . . . there is more. There is also a man much loved and respected by the people. Else why was the trial and journey here conducted in such secrecy?

FORCE: Because . . . . *(Uncertainly)* There might be other traitors around who would try to rescue him.

(HEPHAESTUS *laughs and shakes his head.)*

HEPHAESTUS: And to think it was I who trained you. That is some responsibility!

FORCE: Are you laughing at me, sir?

HEPHAESTUS: Would it make any difference now?

FORCE *(Confused):* I don't understand what you mean.

HEPHAESTUS: Understand this, then. *(Points to* PROMETHEUS, *who groans with pain)* That wretch on whom you would be delighted to do legal murder was a hero, a god. Mothers named their first-born sons after him. Men followed him to the fields and through the streets to catch a word of praise from him, or some suggestion on how to do better. He criticized . . . he inspired. Fine books and great pieces of music were created at his urging . . . .

POWER: And many were directed against the state and its lawful representatives. Eh — How many?

HEPHAESTUS: I am telling you things you should know and remember. I am not *debating* with you!

POWER: No offence . . . I see your point. But . . . .

HEPHAESTUS: But what?

POWER: I think . . . everything happened as it should've. Our government is strong now. The world is at peace. Our First Minister made that clear only last week . . . .

HEPHAESTUS *(Shouting angrily)*: Damn what you think! Chain him to that rock — now!

(Drum beats sound suddenly and continue. POWER *and* FORCE *instantly jump at* PROMETHEUS *and raise him to his feet. They slam him hard against the wall.* PROMETHEUS *coughs and gasps. He stares at* HEPHAESTUS.*)*

HEPHAESTUS *(Furious)*: Yes, it is I! I was always the silent one, yet I, too, am punished by carrying out their will! . . . Damn you, anyway! Son of Themis, who never spoke without thinking — it has come to this — that I must have you chained to a rock like some wild animal. Say something — anything! Curse me . . . or forgive me, I don't care . . . .

*(*PROMETHEUS *only stares at him, his expression frozen.* HEPHAESTUS *struggles for self-control and speaks more quietly.)*

HEPHAESTUS: Your mind will go first from thirst, hunger and loss of blood. You will begin remembering other times . . . not for what they were, but for the false hope they will give you in your growing madness. And all the while, as the minutes of the endless night pass, this cavern with its flames and oozing water will erode you . . . shrinking your painful eyes, bleaching your skin, bloating your flesh and intestines . . . turning the man of intelligence and sensitivity into a monster howling for air, sunlight and morning frost . . . . Why do you not speak to me? Have you forgotten that I, too, was once a man of honour?

*(*PROMETHEUS *is silent.* HEPHAESTUS *writhes.)*

HEPHAESTUS *(Tortured)*: There is no one alive who can save you now — don't you understand? . . . Of the millions of people on earth, only fifty protested outside the courtrooms during your trial. And these surrounded by militia, five hundred strong. That is why you were not condemned to death. Disarmed as you were, they could sentence you to torture in secrecy as an example to others who might find too much sympathy in your arguments for freedom and revolutionary transformation of both man and earth . . . . We have now parted ways, old friend. Still capable of love . . . I think . . . I now have doubts about the holy destiny of people. They have shown themselves capable of selling their own dignity and the dignity of others for a pension plan, or a cool glass of milk on demand! . . . I speak the truth . . . and you must endure what I say in addition to physical pain. Our respected First Minister has decreed you be chained until death, standing on tip-toe!

(PROMETHEUS *laughs bitterly.* FORCE *and* POWER *advance on him, but* HEPHAESTUS *stops them with a motion of his hand.*)

HEPHAESTUS: The saddest sound I have heard today is your laughter, Prometheus.

(HEPHAESTUS *turns away from* PROMETHEUS.)

POWER *(Anxiously):* Why are we waiting for the final order, sir?

HEPHAESTUS: Because I choose to delay . . . .

POWER: I thought our orders from the tribunal were to . . . .

HEPHAESTUS: I know the instructions of the tribunal!

POWER: I'm sorry, sir, but . . . .

HEPHAESTUS: But what? . . . I am an older man than you. We are not stringing up a horse-thief from the old American West here. Let us at least proceed at a dignified pace . . . .

FORCE *(Urgently):* Sir — don't waste pity on him! He's hated by everyone now. They said he was an enemy of progress . . . a maker of wars and discontent.

HEPHAESTUS: He was once a friend.

(PROMETHEUS *laughs bitterly. As if on reflex,* POWER *jumps behind him and wrenches back his head.* PROMETHEUS *groans and shudders in pain.*)

HEPHAESTUS *(Shouts):* Leave him alone!

(*Drum sounds stop.* FORCE *and* POWER *release* PROMETHEUS *and retreat slowly.* PROMETHEUS *sways but remains on his feet. His shackles and bent body project both dignity and humility.*)

POWER *(Shaken):* I do have an obligation to report any irregularities while on duty. I'm not being disrespectful, sir, but I thought you should . . . .

HEPHAESTUS *(Spits with contempt):* What agency of the state is responsible for you, boy?

POWER: Our First Minister was my superior in Internal Security.

HEPHAESTUS: Ah, yes . . . I should have known.

POWER (*Proudly*): He presented me with a medal once, sir. Pinned it here on my chest with his own hands!

HEPHAESTUS: You were rewarded for what? . . . Teaching small children to spy on their parents? . . . Demonstrating eye-gouging?

POWER: No, sir. For marksmanship!

(HEPHAESTUS *snarls with derision*)

HEPHAESTUS: Old men and women tend the fields and orchards now, while youth shoots at things! Do you know the meaning of mercy? Or is hatred all you live for?

FORCE: I don't *hate* . . . . He *knew* he'd get in trouble doing what he did, so he deserves what he's got coming . . . .

POWER: It's nothing to do with me. I'm told what to do.

HEPHAESTUS: How fortunate you are.

POWER: I think I know how you feel, knowing him and all . . . .

HEPHAESTUS: How compassionate of you! (*Storming*) Your orders were to guard him in back of the vehicle. He has serious injuries which he did not have when he was turned over to me!

(POWER *and* FORCE *exchange guarded glances.*)

HEPHAESTUS: Do it then! I am helpless to change what is inevitable . . . .

(POWER *pushes* PROMETHEUS *against rock wall.* PROMETHEUS *stumbles.* FORCE *takes his arm to support him while* POWER *puts his hands under the ribs of* PROMETHEUS *and turns his tortured entrails.* PROMETHEUS *screams in pain, moves helplessly into position. On scream* HEPHAESTUS *covers his ears and turns away.*)

POWER: That's better . . . now to hang this portrait!

(FORCE *laughs as* POWER *takes hammer and steel pegs from his waist-band and begins to hammer the shackles of* PROMETHEUS *into the stone cavern wall. Seeing* HEPHAESTUS *turned away, he leans over and kisses the back of* FORCE*'s neck lasciviously, attempting to hammer without interruption. A hammer blow misses peg and hits* PROMETHEUS *over wrist.* PROMETHEUS *groans and settles as his knees buckle.*)

POWER: None of that! Lift him to his toes.

(Hammering resumes and POWER *and* FORCE *play a vocal game in cadence to hammer blows.)*

POWER: The work . . . .

FORCE: We do . . . .

POWER: Will hold . . . .

FORCE: We must . . . .

POWER: Take care . . . .

FORCE: He has . . . .

POWER: Been known . . . .

FORCE: To . . . .

POWER: Attempt . . . .

FORCE: The . . . .

FORCE AND POWER *(In unison):* Impossible!

*(*HEPHAESTUS *approaches and fearfully checks the binding on the arm of* PROMETHEUS.*)*

HEPHAESTUS: This clasp will last longer than the stone to which it is now anchored!

POWER *(Proudly):* That's right. Now the other arm . . . tightly. Look at him — how quickly all the cleverness is gone now that he's up against the power of our great First Minister of State! The *real* power of the man on top.

HEPHAESTUS: I should be grateful . . . that of all the things I learned in life . . . did not include such skills as these . . . . You will age one day — find yourself helpless. Are you not afraid of memories that are shameful and without pity? You are a slave to what you do!

POWER: We are all slaves, then, sir. Only for the ones on top is there freedom.

HEPHAESTUS: Ah, at least we agree on that.

POWER: Shall we continue?

*(*HEPHAESTUS *seems momentarily transfixed at the gathering fate of* PROMETHEUS *as he looks up at him.)*

POWER: Sir?

HEPHAESTUS *(Startled):* Huh?

POWER: We have allotted time for this job. They will come looking for us if we take too long and it will go badly if there's a complaint!

HEPHAESTUS: We couldn't have that, could we? . . . Proceed. You have my order to proceed . . . . Strange, but a moment ago I saw myself in the final seconds of my life. I was alone . . . abandoned, in a world I did not recognize . . . . And he *(Points to* PROMETHEUS*)* . . . he came through my door . . . *alive!* I was dying and he was alive, and he came to visit me.

*(*POWER *and* FORCE *exchange glances, then turn to* PROMETHEUS.*)*

POWER: Hold up his arm while I hammer this lock shut.

*(*FORCE *wrenches the arm of* PROMETHEUS *upwards with her shoulder.)*

FORCE: Like so?

POWER: That's it.

*(*POWER *strikes a few blows to the lock with his hammer.)*

HEPHAESTUS: How well your work goes. Cold steel over fevered flesh.

POWER: Help her — pull tighter!

*(*HEPHAESTUS *shudders as he touches the arm of* PROMETHEUS *who turns his head to watch him. He helps* FORCE *put the arm in place.)*

POWER: Against the rock . . . hold it tight . . . leave nothing loose. As a young revolutionary, this bastard has been known to escape where no escape was possible!

HEPHAESTUS: This same hand once initialled disarmament agreements and great production programs . . . yet you call him revolutionary and bastard in the same breath. Revolutions are the mother of all civilizations — have you forgotten that in the heat of this . . . this undertaking?

*(*POWER *delivers a few more blows of his hammer to the chaining device, steps back to survey his work with satisfaction.* FORCE *and* HEPHAESTUS *step back from* PROMETHEUS.*)*

POWER: Now the other arm. I think he understands now what a fool he was to contradict the wisdom of our beloved First Minister! *(Fastens other arm)*

HEPHAESTUS: I wish now I had been illiterate in politics and the arts of government.

(POWER *takes a small glittering dagger out of a compartment on his belt and treats it carefully with a chemical. Then with a quick, strong motion he stabs at the upper part of* PROMETHEUS' *stomach.* PROMETHEUS *shouts with pain and rattles the chains securing his arms.* POWER *steps back and wipes his dagger. Blood covers the stomach of* PROMETHEUS.)

POWER *(a bit unsteady):* That's one procedure I don't care for. It's reserved for the most stubborn ones.

HEPHAESTUS: What is it?

POWER: It's called the Tongue of Jupiter . . . .

POWER: Blade is made of special alloy for this . . . coated with chemicals which burn like fire, yet won't kill or let him faint. I don't care for it myself, but the lab in my unit is sure proud of this one.

(POWER *replaces dagger.* HEPHAESTUS *moves into shadows and retches.* POWER *turns on him angrily.*)

POWER: I said I didn't care for it! What more's there to say? . . . It might even help him to die quicker . . . or bring out the sewer rats for the blood, which will be the same thing . . . .

HEPHAESTUS: What in hell are you saying?

POWER: Would you like to run out to the waiting truck and take off? Because this was once your friend? To me he's an enemy of the state and the people. Just remember that, or you might end up joining him here!

HEPHAESTUS: Don't you speak to me that way! We are dealing in horror now, not just politics!

POWER: I was never a Deputy so I know nothing about that, and I couldn't care less. I receive convicts and do what I'm told . . . more even, so there's no complaints from anyone. To me he's just an uppity convict who lost out . . . . Now for the belt around his waist . . . . Here, pull!

(*He offers* HEPHAESTUS *one end of heavy belt which he carries over the mid-section of the writhing* PROMETHEUS. HEPHAESTUS *does not obey.* FORCE *steps forward.*)

FORCE: I'll help . . . .

POWER: Not you. *(Coldly)* He helps!

HEPHAESTUS: Do it yourselves. I do not take orders from you.

(POWER stares cruelly at HEPHAESTUS, then laughs sarcastically.)

POWER: I have orders to take over in this place. Which means I get help when I ask for it. If not, I write out a report on what went wrong and why — I put an "urgent" sticker on it and it goes right up to the top in the agency . . . . You want that to happen, sir? . . . Lock his legs with this!

(With contempt, he throws a leg iron and chain towards HEPHAESTUS, who slowly picks it up, examines it, and clasps it on legs of PROMETHEUS.)

POWER: Tighter! Lock them tighter!

(Reluctantly HEPHAESTUS obeys.)

POWER: I've never had a prisoner escape — did you know that?

(HEPHAESTUS stares at him icily.)

POWER: I've never had a prisoner escape because I know my job . . . same's her. I do my job well. I was trained that way. 'Persist, but don't rush,' said our instructor in intelligence work.

FORCE: He also said, 'If you apply some imagination you can break the spirit.'

HEPHAESTUS: Imagination? What is imaginative about cruelty?

POWER *(Mocking him):* What a soft heart! . . . How have you managed to survive to your age in this world? And in the security service of all places! Is this how you earned your big home in the country? Your servants? A staff car? Your pension benefits?

HEPHAESTUS: Enough!

POWER: It's not enough! *(Sneering)* You're an aging whore with loose teeth, old man, sir!

(PROMETHEUS laughs. HEPHAESTUS clenches his fists in fury, then turns away from his tormentors. POWER lunges at PROMETHEUS and strikes him across the face. FORCE jumps close behind POWER, as in a combat reflex, her hands clenching and unclenching.)

POWER: Even now . . . here . . . he is still insolent! *(To HEPHAESTUS)* In the back of the garbage truck . . . on the way here . . . he sang . . . wouldn't stop singing. So we worked him over a bit. I said

I'd kill him if he didn't stop. He turned to me and you know what he said? . . . He said that he could never die . . . that he . . . was beyond death!

(HEPHAESTUS *stares at* PROMETHEUS *and moves away in horror.*)

HEPHAESTUS: Oh, my god!

POWER *(To* PROMETHEUS*):* But we've got you for bats and sewer rats to take apart! The tribunal called you Prometheus the contriver and the world spits on you! . . . So contrive all you want — nobody knows where you are and nobody cares. Not now . . . . Not ever again! Make trouble and you get trouble!

(PROMETHEUS *tugs violently at his constraints. They hum and clatter.* POWER *laughs, then turns away and, taking* FORCE *by her arm, both exit in a military goose-step.* HEPHAESTUS *lingers, his hand over his eyes.* PROMETHEUS *groans and* HEPHAESTUS *shudders.*)

(Drum beats)

PROMETHEUS *(Singing):*
> Oh, winds from the icy mountains
> And river waters enslaved by hills
> Before the final roar of freedom
> In the ocean waves — Oh, sweet earth
> Beneath the ageless sun who sees
> The sum total of all suffering.

(HEPHAESTUS *turns and exits at a run.*)

PROMETHEUS *(Raging in cadence to drums):*
> See me and the tortures I am
> Condemned to endure by those
> Profiteers and false commisars
> Who rose as flotsam to the top
> Addressing each other by first name
> Exchanging cars, suits and advice
> On conquest of the earth and stars —
> Who hears me now, entombed in the bowels
> Of this raging planet? And from
> What corner of the heavens
> Shall deliverance come?
>
> Not from peaceful deliberations
> Shall the great changes come —
> Not now — even were I blind

There would be no mistaking
The howling torment of the future
Built on betrayals of the past —
Built on rivers of spilled revolutionary blood,
These new perversions of the ageless game
Continue, and honest men cannot be silent
When human dignity is spat upon
And the very mention of a peoples' destiny
Is blasphemous unless it is
Officially approved . . . .

(Over drum sounds, distant rumble of heavy traffic or disturbance above the cavern. One of the flames from broken pipe flares high momentarily, then dies back.)

PROMETHEUS:

In dark caves and secret places
I have, from the authority of high office,
Helped maintain the sacred flame of honour
And ongoing struggle for perfectibility
And resurrection of the human will
Against tired men grown old too soon
And burdened with their comforts
And fearsome acquisitions . . .
Foremost among these is he
Who rose to the highest pinnacle
Of power on the yearnings
Of the people, only to betray
The masses with false fear
Of war and hunger — and the terrors
Of a long winter without heat —
He thus conspired to blunt and dull
The rightful wishes of the earth's poor
For bread, land and freedom.
Such decaying leaders fortify each other
And in time the rich grow richer
Than entire nations
While the poor — more numerous now —
Fade into a gray landscape of despair
Without voice or hope — all calls
For action now quickly savaged
With contempt, prison, long years
Of exile from events and family . . .
The profile of slavery is this:

Deny protein to a man and feed him sugars.
Then withdraw these slowly — what remains
Is now a slave without mind or motivation;
A sluggard sitting by the roadside
Staring with unseeing eyes at wars, pillage,
Dismemberment of his own household
Which leave him unperturbed, untouched
In a dreamy world only troubled
By chill-spasms when the blood cries for
And is denied — more sugar!
What horror do I see in this
Reflection of the human spirit?
What horror do I hear?
The beat of dripping wings, the sigh
Of cavern winds, blowing from the deepest,
Darkest, most cold and melancholy
Depths of earth beneath the sea . . . .

(Drum sounds stop abruptly. FARMER *and* WORKER *enter, dressed in cave-explorers' apparel.)*

WORKER: The sounds came from here . . . . Look!

(He lights the body and face of PROMETHEUS *with a flashlight.)*

FARMER: It's Prometheus, the Deputy! Who in hell has done this!

PROMETHEUS:
Go away! I have no patience
For killers and torturers
Sent into the bowels of this earth
To bury the mistakes of savages
Who've seized the helm of government!

FARMER: We knew nothing of this. There were rumours you'd been detained, and then nothing more.

WORKER: A great man of the people — and then this! Why? Who did it? . . . We'll release you and treat your wounds, Prometheus.

PROMETHEUS: The sharpest chisels in the world could not cut me free now — go away!

FARMER: You were our second in command once . . . I remember how good it felt to hear debates on every street corner about questions long suppressed in the interest of national security . . . .

PROMETHEUS:

> Why is it that every traitor
> Hides first in the shadows
> Of national security?
> *(Suspiciously)*
> But you have come to gloat and taunt me!
> You have come on his orders . . . I know
> The ruse!

(PROMETHEUS *struggles helplessly in his chains, then subsides.*)

FARMER: What orders? Had we taken another turn in the cave network back there, we'd never have found you here. Prometheus, is it true, this rumour of violence you planned against the state?

PROMETHEUS:

> Not the state . . . but against
> A certain military unit I had once
> Voted to create as special protection
> For key people in the government . . .
> But they exist! Foolishly, I created them and
> Encouraged friends of good will to man them. This
> Cavern was their first research facility . . . .
> Now, their guns and spies are turned on simple people
> Who might have a question or a doubt
> About where this new order and its leader
> Plan to take this gentle land
> And all who love it.

FARMER: I understand your anger and your pain, Prometheus. I understand. Somehow your love and care for all of us was subverted by enemies of the country, though how I'll never understand.

PROMETHEUS:

> Enough! I'll hear no more of this!
> Sooner would I wither on this rock
> Or be flung from one spearing outcrop
> To the next in blind darkness
> By a massive earthquake, or freeze
> In dark winds which issue from some frozen
> River under earth, than listen one more time
> To such perjury!

WORKER: We are not perjurers, Prometheus. The laws we have made are the laws by which we live.

PROMETHEUS:
> They have become laws
> Of vengeance and oppression!

FARMER: Your torment is a sad thing to accept. And even if we don't speak about it, we suspect the First Minister of State has overstepped his limits a bit in recent times. And that is a sad thing to accept.

PROMETHEUS:
> Overstepped his limits, you say?
> He has gained a clawhold on an empire for it!
> But that is not enough — not for him.
> I saw him driven by fear
> To sniff at the quality of love professed
> For him — searching for doubt,
> Mistrust—scribblings on the washroom walls—
> Sensing plots to rob him of honour and his throne.
> First, I am befriended by a heavy-breathing
> Host of petty-thieves turned body-guards
> For weekend visits to secluded villas
> For urgent consultations on matters
> Pertaining to the state.
> These turned out nothing but excuses
> For moody drinking and excessive eating —
> I criticize, but keep my anger to myself.
> Then I am threatened
> For having knowledge of plots being devised
> From the outside world.
> I am charged in secret, tried and convicted
> To this torture, which has stabbed his back
> As well as mine, with fear of darker times
> To come . . . .

WORKER: There is gossip now of a woman close to you and the First Minister . . . that a personal argument has somehow become political. Is this true?

(PROMETHEUS *turns away from them, his face tortured.*)

FARMER: Is it true, Prometheus? The people will forgive you if they know the truth . . . I've served my time in the armed forces . . . I know second-hand the horrors of torture and pain. What they've done to you is more than that, and I'm not afraid to speak about it to my friends and to organizations of people. But your return will be slow, acceptance of your blame and forgiveness will take time.

WORKER: What he says is true. At this moment, no land on earth would give you refuge and no god forgive you until your good name is cleared. I'm sorry, Prometheus, but that's the way it is . . . .

PROMETHEUS: The plotting of my personal destruction
Has been more thorough than I thought . . . .

WORKER: Yes. And it's not helped by your defiance.

PROMETHEUS: *(Anxious)*
        Yet he, and those who planned it so
        Are few in numbers — they fill a modest room!
        Their ships at sea, aircraft in the sky,
        Rocketry and chemistry of war
        Makes nations tremble at their word
        Or angry glance of eye —
        They fill a modest room
        These power brokers of the universe,
        Small men obsessed with assurances
        Of honours, medals minted in their names,
        Finer food and clothing than their peers —
        Mention of their prowess
        On the holy days of state —
        How fearful is their pride!

FARMER: Yet you were one of them — and until this moment you were silent. Maybe it's too late . . . .

PROMETHEUS:
        I erred, but it's not too late.
        For he, who is now First Minister
        Must in time bow to the same adversities
        Which overcome us all.
        In times to come
        I see him in my inner eye
        Approach me, imploring friendship
        And forgiveness . . . .

WORKER: If that happens, what will you do?

PROMETHEUS:
        I was tried and convicted of subversion
        On orders of the man whom I nominated

For the highest office in our land,
Of this early error I am guilty.
When our previous leader died
There was much discord and hostile nations
Fostered various factions of the masses into conflict
So they might at an opportune time intervene
In our affairs in the name of peace
And dismember our achievements and our wealth
For their own profit.

WORKER: We live with that threat . . . .

PROMETHEUS:

Knowing this, and sensing factions
Even in our armed forces
I counselled as best I knew,
Coaxing the timid, holding back the headstrong,
Passing up great talents in politics
In favour of the weak —
All in the interests of internal peace . . . .

FARMER: For which the people thank you.

PROMETHEUS:

Our present First Minister
Was a compromise in which I saw
Good merit and much to recommend him,
And so the new tyrant was awakened
From his fitful sleep —
It is not for this that I oppose him,
But for his brutal insolence
And his choice of council
From the dregs of criminality,
Futile, ineffectual beings,
Which began the process of creating
A strange new human in our midst —
Noisy adventurers, shouters of slogans,
Small minds viewing all the problems of commerce,
Culture and international affairs
Through the narrow window
Of a lowland village barn . . .
For this I am condemned to lingering death,
The antidote to freedom!

WORKER: In the army and among the people, you are the symbol of the revolution, the living legacy of a better life to come. How sad to see this ending.

PROMETHEUS *(Angry):*
> Return to your work, then!
> I ask for soldiers, not pall-bearers . . .
> I will not be pitied!

FARMER: When I was a child, my father taught me that life conquers death, that light conquers darkness. That neither slavery nor despair are natural to living people. When I asked him how he knew this, he said Prometheus told him it was so.

PROMETHEUS *(Struggling against his shackles):*
> Return to your work, I say!
> I demand action, not blind hope!

WORKER: You're the only hope we have. We cannot turn against you, no matter what you've done. You gave fire to the spirit of us all.

PROMETHEUS:
> The same fire imprisons me now.
> It was workers like yourself,
> Who, without protest or question
> Made the alloy for these chains I wear . . .
> Which a thousand others wore before me!

FARMER: Surely you knew of this . . . did you protest? What were we to do, who knew nothing?

(PROMETHEUS *is startled by the question.)*

PROMETHEUS:
> Do the people still believe
> In the resurrection of the spirit?

WORKER: Peasants, soldiers, workers in the mills . . . they are still the same people you worked and moved among when you had time for us.

PROMETHEUS: And what have they learned?

WORKER: I don't understand.

PROMETHEUS:
> Where were the voices of the people
> When these outrageous trials were held

With public charges and secret testimony?
Even nations who regard us
With contempt and hatred
For igniting skulls and human tallow
With new hope in a dying world
Regard such happenings with sorrow —
Such grief means nothing to me.
The indifference of my countrymen
Is the greatest torture I have yet endured.

(WORKER *and* FARMER *turn away in shame.*)

WORKER: We were afraid . . . what can I say?

PROMETHEUS:

Afraid? *(Snarling)*
It was a grovelling act of shame
That lacked even the dignity of death-fear
Which I had trained you once
To overcome!

FARMER: I once thought I was a man of purpose, but not now. How long ago it seems that we all marched behind you, hungry, yet so happy in knowing we were changing history. We felt we'd never die so long as Prometheus was our leader. Now this god is chained . . . a slave to the very thing we bled to save and give life to!

WORKER: If we said you'd asked forgiveness . . . .

PROMETHEUS *(Sadly):*

Thirst and pain plays havoc
With the mind . . . I see before me now
Gentle fields and sloping valleys of my childhood
Where as a country boy I pondered
On the free flight of swallows
In the summer sky . . .
How simple in such circumstance
To scold those tormented with adversity . . . .

WORKER: I suggested it because I worry for you.

PROMETHEUS:

In the fever of reshaping destiny
I ignored this time, this place,
And the possibility I might occupy
The chains of others

Whose names and faces
Were unknown and of no concern
To me . . . so return to work, friends,
And think of troubled days to come.
Have compassion but not pity for me.
No apologies or compromises
I once sanctioned . . .
The years ahead are times of struggle
And remorse — such is our lot.

FARMER: There's little hope for my lifetime if what you say is true, Prometheus.

WORKER: Is it you, or we, who are being crucified? *(With anger)* Tell us! I want to know what's beyond this short life racing by me!

(A roar and shriek of some machine grows louder and stops. The ADMIRAL *enters. There is a flash of white flame and a dying sputter. He turns in direction from which he has entered, a confused, worried expression on his face.* ADMIRAL *sees* FARMER *and* WORKER, *and becomes agitated.)*

ADMIRAL: What in hell are you doing here? This place is off limits to civilians — how'd you get in? Never mind — get out or I'll have my pilot slam you into cages so small they'll bend you four ways to fit you in! Out!

*(*WORKER *and* FARMER *retreat and exit.)*

*(*ADMIRAL *glances at* PROMETHEUS *and does a bizarre and unexpected little dance, which might be motivated by need for exercise or nervousness.)*

ADMIRAL: Ah, Prometheus . . . .

PROMETHEUS *(Mocking):* Ah, Admiral!

ADMIRAL: I've come to see you . . . come on this new machine which travels under water, on land and in the air as smooth as a limousine! You made it happen, sir . . . others have forgotten, but not me, that it was you who said 'without technology we'll walk on one leg, like cripples!' Smart, very smart!

*(*PROMETHEUS *coughs uncomfortably.)*

ADMIRAL: I heard about the mess you're in at the Chiefs of Staff meeting. Twisted some arms to find out where you were . . . .

PROMETHEUS: What for?

ADMIRAL: We've been friends a long time . . . knew each other as cadets — wasn't that where it started?

PROMETHEUS: Such things escape my mind . . . .

ADMIRAL: This is bad business, Prometheus . . . and don't take that to mean I sympathize with you. Not bloody likely. I'll speak to you simply, as a common man . . . because my eyes hear, my ears can see.

(ADMIRAL *hesitates, realizing it is not correct.* PROMETHEUS *laughs.*)

PROMETHEUS:

>As cadets, all of us surpassed you
>In examinations for training of cadres
>To which you responded —
>"I don't think. I do."
>It now seems your life has been
>A vindication of this credo.

(ADMIRAL *is puzzled by the barb he cannot locate. Off-stage machine flares and sputters again. It distracts the* ADMIRAL.)

ADMIRAL: Why in hell can't he keep his hands off the controls? I told him to park it and wait . . . . Where was I?

PROMETHEUS: Heaven only knows . . . .

ADMIRAL: Oh yes, I speak simply and don't flatter, yet this uniform carries weight when it matters. (*Startled by his own poetic eloquence*) How was I going to put it? . . . Our beloved First Minister and I are just like that! (*Holds up his hand with two crossed fingers*)

PROMETHEUS: Which one of you is on top?

ADMIRAL: He's on top . . . it's his right.

(PROMETHEUS *laughs.*)

ADMIRAL: If you want me to speak to him for you, you just give the word. I don't turn my back on a friend. Others might, but not this fella!

PROMETHEUS:

>What is this I look upon?
>In your polyester uniform, tailored
>To disguise the curses of advancing age —
>Fat jowled, driven by machines of war
>Like some primordial, dim-witted god!

ADMIRAL: Now you just hold on a minute!

(PROMETHEUS *stares at him, an expression of amazement on his face.*)

PROMETHEUS: You've a remarkable talent for the obvious.

ADMIRAL: What you think is not my business. I'd never agree with anything you say — officially. As far as I'm concerned, you're a traitor and deserve to rot here. Unofficially, you keep a watch on your tongue and I'll work to arrange another hearing for you to get out of this . . . this cesspool.

PROMETHEUS *(Hesitant, moved):*
> I marvel at you,
> Indeed I do . . . that you have known me
> Yet kept your distance in the public eye —
> A true soldier.
> I advise you to remain that way.
> Your petition for a new hearing
> Might jeopardize the safety
> you've enjoyed so long.

ADMIRAL: Appreciate that . . . always have, you know. I'm not the fool you think. I've got a common man's cunning. Our navy has sobered the leaders of more productive countries than ours. So my word goes a long way even with the likes of our First Minister. He may laugh behind my back at the way I look and speak . . . I know he does . . . but he's never sure which command I'll disregard. I'll be heard, be sure of that, and your freedom will come, give or take some time.

PROMETHEUS: Be careful, Admiral.

ADMIRAL: You be careful. War is my profession.

PROMETHEUS:
> If you knew as do I the other agencies of state
> Who prowl by night, spying on those
> Who labour for the common good — compiling dossiers,
> Forcing dismissals, setting fires to hard-earned
> Personal possessions — creating accidents on lonely roads,
> Arranging disappearances
> All for reasons nobody recalls — but our new tyrant
> Knows the power of these forces
> For he rose to power through them.

ADMIRAL: It strikes me strange that here you're at war, while I, the warrior, look for ways to end such violence . . . . What you say and do in these times is dangerous for all of us. I hope things will cool down a bit when you're free again.

PROMETHEUS: There is not the remotest hope for that!

ADMIRAL: Prometheus — think before you speak! The land and people are so tired now. What's happened to the simple truth we had as youth? Was it not enough? Since the revolution we've been torn by schisms, which you helped create, I think. We've been preoccupied by real and imagined traitors. I understand and appreciate all you've done for technology and culture, but where's our joy gone?

PROMETHEUS:
> The joy is in the struggle!
> The destination is infinite!
> If you don't understand this
> Then you've wasted your time
> Seeing me!

ADMIRAL *(Angry):* You are chained like an animal that bites, Prometheus! Listen to what I say — I'm not a dog barking at the wind!

PROMETHEUS:
> You came with sorrow
> And I give you bitterness.
> That is not much of an exchange.

ADMIRAL: It's not my love or hatred for you that's keeping you hanging on the wall of a cave, goddammit! . . . It's something else which I don't understand.

PROMETHEUS:
> Then obey orders from those who do
> If a natural death means anything to you.
> What else can I say?

ADMIRAL: I guess . . . there's no more to be said.

PROMETHEUS:
> It was good of you to come.
> Hearing what you think
> Reassures me.

ADMIRAL: I wish times were happier . . . . I'm going back in a machine that rides on air and water so smoothly I can sleep when I travel. I'll think of you . . . here . . . I wish the times were happier . . . .

(ADMIRAL *departs quickly. Offstage, his machine roars to life. Sound recedes on his departure. Enter* FARMER *and* WORKER, *passing before and around* PROMETHEUS *in a choreography of grief. They chant.*)

FARMER: He's been taken to hang below the earth, his flesh a damp banner — his eyes, a raging storm. And I, simple man of the earth and sun, weep helplessly for him — at the might and wealth these hands have helped to build.

WORKER: From Tehran to Buenos Aires, Washington to Vladivostok, the earth cries and shudders for Prometheus, friend of life and liberator of the spirit. Tyranny, once conquered, now sprouts like some rank weed . . . .

FARMER: These hands have planted food. And helped build the instruments of war from which I cringe. Those who make a mockery of me exult in war — their gunbarrels placed and aimed in swamps, on oceans and among the stars . . . .

WORKER: Soldiers! Think before you shoot! Listen to the groan of him who struggled to relieve you of the burden of warfare.

FARMER: Bent in toil on my fields side by side with my wife, who holds up half the heavens, he shares my suffering and I his, but here we differ. My concern is for an acre of this earth while his is for the black void of the universe . . . .

WORKER: Earth, sky and dark places underneath the sea are struggling with his pain . . . . Still his deepest anguish is the silence of the people forced to swallow half an argument. Give us ammunition for your defense, Prometheus!

PROMETHEUS:
> It is not because of insolence or pride
> I kept my peace — I could have called
> For protests and cries of outrage
> Were it not for the guilt I carry.

WORKER: What guilt?

PROMETHEUS:
> It was my persuasion which swayed votes
> In favour of the new tyrant, who,
> In his first days in office

Dared rewrite the constitution.
I did not age growing older
But willingly accepted, too willingly,
The fast solutions of my youth
To complex problems centuries in the making.
Like the hunter, having killed something
I felt better. I did not
Become a pall-bearer to the past; instead,
I flung myself headlong into problems
Of the reconstruction.
Not all that fell was dead — some bodies
Healed and rose again, donned the dress
And manners of the revolution and proceeded
To exchange barnyard security of slaves
Against the chilly promise of a freedom
Only dimly understood . . . .
To exchange death for life —
Ignorance for reason — prisons for debate . . .
To exchange dead gods
For unimaginative but living men . . .
Too much credence did I place
On human progress.

WORKER: What you say is true . . . . Many changes shook our lives. At first, everything was debated in the streets and at places where the people worked. But with the passing years we were only told what had been decided by our leaders. Your name appeared on some of these directives.

PROMETHEUS: Yes.

WORKER: Truth, in which we took such pride once, became a matter of who spoke first. Debate became an unfamiliar language known only to a few. News of scandal was like a hidden bait. The morals of people we once worshipped were clouded — to this day there is a whisper of some woman you betrayed.

PROMETHEUS:

Leave her out of this!
She will not be used
To shadow more serious
Matters which affect us all!

WORKER: I believe in you, will obey you. But I must know what's expected of me, and if I've failed in reaching expectations you had for me . . . .

136

(PROMETHEUS *struggles with discomfort.*)

PROMETHEUS:
      Forgive me, but I've heard such sentiments
      Before when it served their needs!

(WORKER *and* FARMER *step back, shocked.*)

PROMETHEUS:
      How much of the duplicity of which you speak
      Did you willingly accept?
      Did you really understand my undertaking
      In creating love for learning?
      My concerns for deep studies of medicine
      And science to liberate simple people
      From their fears of pain and insecurity
      And harnessing their fascination
      With mysteries of heavens
      And the earth below their feet?

FARMER: Look at you . . . a god among men, dressed in rags, homeless . . . .

PROMETHEUS:
      My freedom is some years away
      But I shall be delivered from this bondage.
      As for other things . . . .

WORKER (*Interrupting*): Delivered by whom?

PROMETHEUS:
      By necessity. The men
      Who welded chains
      About my wrists feel
      They have inherited a world
      Where all can go into the deepest
      Sleep. That machines will run machines,
      To manufacture arms, shirts
      And predigested foods,
      With indifference to the raging storms
      Brewing in the cosmos.

WORKER: Are these storms you speak of greater than those envisioned by our present leaders?

PROMETHEUS:

>For a time he will rule
>Guarded by armed forces,
>The new constitution
>And the silence of workers
>Who confuse liberty with a well-stocked
>Department store.
>*(Smiles)* Even as we speak this way
>The earth has turned and aged.

WORKER: You know you can trust us. If there's something we should know or do . . . .

PROMETHEUS:

>I will not speak of the time
>Or conditions of release
>From my outrage and humiliation.
>The cage our First Minister
>Forged for me
>Will in time close around him.
>Arguments he employed for my condemnation
>Will return like ravens
>Clawing at his face.

FARMER *(Angry):* I'm a worker in the fields, producing food for philosophers, bootmakers, miners, children, thieves, sailors and all others. I'm a peaceful man, giving thanks to whatever guards my health and the health of fields I cultivate . . . .

WORKER: And I, a worker, thank heaven for my right to labour, for my children and my precious leisure. Yet I return to this place with danger to myself, for the long, damp night of your fall, Prometheus, is a turning point in my own fortune. I'm afraid of mighty men who rise from troubled times . . . .

PROMETHEUS: What is there to fear now?

WORKER: Your faith in the final wisdom of ordinary people. Men and women who fought alongside of you . . . many of these would now turn against you out of fear.

PROMETHEUS: You lie!

FARMER: What courage have I, or my friends, against the machines and power built in my name and honour, and now turned against me? I'm weak, blinded by my private dreams of peace. Why do you not let me rest, even if my serenity is an illusion for a short while?

(IO *enters, her movements distracted, confused, as she searches for a way out of the cavern.* ARGUS *also enters and follows her woodenly, his face that of a dead man. He makes notes of her activities. When she draws near him, he becomes agitated, excited. But she is conscious of this reaction, and paces her movements away from him.* ARGUS *is visible only to* IO.)

WORKER: Or me? . . . You are dying, and a part of me dies with you. I followed you to life. I did not ask for death!

(PROMETHEUS *turns away from them.*)

WORKER (*Angry, disturbed*): Don't turn from me. I left my place of work to dance with my wife and children at your wedding!

(PROMETHEUS *strains at his shackles, a moan of pain rising from his lips.*)

IO (*In pleading tones*):
    Who can tell me where I am?
    What people live here
    In this bat-infested, steaming cavern?
    Why is this man chained like some beast?
    What crimes are possible
    For such a monstrous punishment?
    Or is this a vision of my own
    Final hours of my life?
    Tell me, someone!

(WORKER *and* FARMER *turn away from her.* PROMETHEUS *is torn between recognition and dismay. She turns to each of them, pleading.*)

IO (*Pointing to* ARGUS):
    A dead spy
    Working for God alone knows
    What state or economic power
    Has driven me across this earth and back!
    He's dead . . . I know he's dead
    For with this hand
    I killed him . . . . Twice shot him
    through the heart — him,
    Who made of me a whore . . .
    Begged and paid me to haunt
    Bedrooms of the world's powerful men,
    Trading lust for information

On movements of commerce, secret research
And the private fears of statesmen.
I killed him, but the earth
Expelled his body, and now
He pursues me night and day
As does the banishment
By the leader of this country
Who forgives nothing . . .
I wish to die, yet cannot.
I wish to sleep, but dare not
Close my eyes for fear his icy hands
Will brush my face, my breasts . . . .

(She stares at PROMETHEUS, *but does not recognize him.)*

IO:

I cannot see you for my tears
And the rank shadows of this place . . .
Yet I sense a god in pain
Greater than my own.

*(*PROMETHEUS *is agitated.)*

PROMETHEUS *(Softly):*

Io . . . it has come to this
For you?

(A rumble of an earthquake. Burning lights flare and sputter. IO *screams and turns.* ARGUS *grabs her and laughs mirthlessly as he tries to lock his body against hers. She tears away and tries to hide behind* WORKER *and* FARMER, *but* ARGUS *blocks her escape.* PROMETHEUS *struggles against his chains in rage.)*

IO: You know me? No one knows me now!

PROMETHEUS:

How can I forget? . . . I would remember you
Even when all else had left my mind!

IO:

No one knows me
Except torturers and paid assassins
Who at intervals place my body
On their racks, then fling it
To the far horizon in a speeding
Car or train, to be thrown

> On brutal pavement of deserted roads
> Or down the slopes of jagged hillsides
> Where I choke and cry with pain —
> I cannot die, I rise again.

(She points to ARGUS *and whimpers.)*

PROMETHEUS: It is I . . . Prometheus.

(She refuses to believe him. Backs away from him.)

IO:

> No! . . . Prometheus is at the capital
> Absorbed in work which moves the earth,
> I must not think of him . . .
> My mind is dying . . . I've tried
> Not to think of him . . . it is
> Seven years since I last saw him . . .
> I must not . . . .

FARMER: This is Prometheus, Io. This is Prometheus in front of us, hanging from steel pegs like some broken animal!

IO:

> No! When we were
> Together, his health
> Ignited all about him — his spirit
> Was like some overflowing field
> Rich with warm and splendid things!

PROMETHEUS: Those days and nights are gone, Io.

(She approaches him in growing recognition and horror.)

IO: You? Here? . . . This way?

*(*PROMETHEUS *nods, unable to meet her gaze.)*

IO:

> Dearest Prometheus, who reduced you
> To such wretchedness?

PROMETHEUS:

> It was done on command of our illustrious
> Head of state — executed by the blacksmith
> Of the secret service — Hephaestus.
> *(Laughs)* In some previous life
> Those two might have been farriers
> In a smithy!

(IO *comes up to* PROMETHEUS, *and rising on tip-toe brushes his cheeks with her hands.*)

IO:

Neither you nor I can die
Of pain or punishments!

PROMETHEUS: I wish you had been spared all this.

IO:

I did not leave you, Prometheus —
I waited for you . . . am prepared to wait
For all eternity . . . .
For what crimes are you so punished?

PROMETHEUS:

My answer would change nothing.
Let us speak of other things.

IO:

I did not plan this meeting.
I was travelling blindly, as I do,
Through nights and days, following
Dark lanes and tunnels in the earth.

WORKER: A good woman deserves pity for such torment . . . but *her?*
She was once your wife, Prometheus. And now she's branded as
a whore and spy by all the nations! She has no allegiance to a man
or place on earth . . . . What is to be done with someone like her?

IO (*Clutching her head*): No!

(FARMER *comes to her side and supports her.*)

FARMER: We've seen too many easy condemnations. I'd like to hear
her story.

(PROMETHEUS *struggles with anguish in his chains.*)

PROMETHEUS:

I've denied such rumours
Knowing how easy it is to condemn
Yet you left me, Io.

IO: I did what I did out of love for you!

PROMETHEUS:

Let them be your judges, for these men
Are brothers to us both.

142

Nothing is lost on such jurors,
Innocence will still draw
Tears in this icy desert
Of the soul!

(The melody of IO*'s theme song is heard being whistled in background.)*

IO:

I did not leave you, Prometheus.
I only left the home we shared
And which I could not bear alone.
I tried to find you, but each hour and day
Made the distance to you greater.
Seldom did I see you after
The first whisperings of morning.

PROMETHEUS: It was only temporary.

IO:

It was years, Prometheus!
Agonizing years of loneliness.
I was young . . . green as meadowlands
Where my father tended cattle
White as first snows of winter.
When you walked the street of our village
Urging agricultural reform
You were a god to me — glowing
As the first light of day.
Honeybees crowded for your breath
And wild birds, dazzled by your eyes
And smile, dove above you like squadrons
Of love-dazed airborne guards
Protecting you not wisely
But with deepest love.
We met, and in my father's house
You stayed for dinner of the sweetest bread,
Red meat and wine from vineyards
Of the village . . . .
*(*IO *turns to* FARMER *and* WORKER*)*
We were comrades and lovers, he and I,
Wandering by day into remotest valleys,
Convincing the dubious, organizing
The distrustful into enthusiastic bands
Of men reborn!
By night we shared what crumbs we had

> And lay side by side, his wondrous aura
> Covering us with warmth . . . .

(She turns away and sobs. FARMER *and* WORKER *comfort her. She continues, but avoids looking at the tortured face of* PROMETHEUS.*)*

IO:

> The revolutionary council summoned him
> To the troubled northern regions . . . he left,
> And I, crazed by his love, lonely,
> Devoured by his touch and kiss, waited.
> For three years I lived for his letters
> And news of him from travelling emissaries,
> Then went in search of him —
> In search of him, to the deepest reaches
> Of hell itself I went!
> My face, glowing with the passions
> Which I carried in me, excited
> Battalions of men — saints and demons
> Both ran beside me, panting their desires,
> Lavishing their gifts at me —
> Inviting betrayal.
> The goat stench of men in heat
> Was forever on the breeze
> Which blew my way . . . .

(Points to ARGUS.*)*

IO *(In rage):*

> He, the devil incarnate
> Reached me with the most monstrous
> Promise of them all! He promised me
> Prometheus again, and I,
> The country fool, believed him.

(She hesitates, confused, as she stares at the grinning ARGUS.*)*

FARMER: What happened then, child?

IO:

> What followed, the very rivers of the earth
> Will never wash away — the degradation
> Of the harlot, denunciation by my father
> And my sister —
> The sweaty labourings o'er my body
> Of the man who at this moment

Commands all power in this nation.
(With a self-condemning cry)
Yes, even him! And when I fled
He unleashed the full fury
Of his vengeance with a roar,
"Prometheus a better man than I?
Heaven and hell together
Will not save him now!"
Argus, whom I killed
Was resurrected from his grave
To haunt me, and the whips of all states
Were bared to lash my back and buttocks
As I passed, until welcome madness
Numbed me.

(She whimpers and withdraws like a child under the protective arm of the FARMER. PROMETHEUS throws his head in fury. Slowly, he subsides and looks down at her, his expression one of remorse.)

PROMETHEUS:

The village of your birth, in twilight
Was like burnished bronze.
Warm light rising from scant earth
And shadows like dark cloaks
Followed lowing cattle homeward bound.

IO:

On such hours of the dying days
I gathered eggs for you.

PROMETHEUS:

In times to come
Roads and rivers shall
Be named for you . . . .

IO:

Nightly I waited for you
In my father's garden
Crickets chirping in the trees
Children's laughter and music
Filling lanes and doorways
Each night I waited for you.

PROMETHEUS: But you are well? You hear my voice?

(She laughs suddenly and dances away from FARMER and WORKER.)

IO:

>Oh, this is the happiest of all times!
>The changing of the seasons
>Takes my breath away, and all the . . .

PROMETHEUS *(Forcefully):*

>Say no more!
>"This is the happiest of all times," she says,
>Then turns away from me
>As if startled by some sound
>Or sudden stab of pain . . . .

(She hears him and retreats toward FARMER *and* WORKER, *as if for shelter from what may follow.)*

IO *(Fearfully):*

>Tell me it is not true!
>That I have gone blind and see
>Strange images in the mirror
>Of the inner eye . . .
>It is a dream and nothing more —
>He is a great man still
>Changing history, and not chained
>In some damp, decaying cave
>Like a savage beast!

PROMETHEUS:

>Speak no more
>Of children's play times
>Or flowers
>In the wakening fields
>When your mind and mine
>Is still aglow
>From the flaming shelter
>Of the last April moon
>We shared
>In another world
>Ten thousand miles
>From this place . . .
>Let us speak instead
>Of how very, very civil
>It is to meet this way
>As strangers selling land
>Or enquiring for the park

Without touch
Or unexpected joy . . .
Say no more
Of things we knew as children
In another life.
Let us speak instead
Of the passing of the days and hours
And sacrifices of the soul.

(IO *is stung and touched by what he says. She moves to him, past* ARGUS, *whom she now pushes aside.*)

IO:

I would not have wished it this way,
Not for you — not for myself.

FARMER: It's sad to hear such words from her.

PROMETHEUS: You are given to quick sorrow, friend!

FARMER *(Stung):* How can you not feel pity for her here where the very stones weep for us all?

PROMETHEUS: I no longer have patience for submission!

IO:

I would not have wished it this way . . .
Many days I dreamed of a simple life
Of few possessions, quiet thoughts
And hours filled with labour for others
And ourselves.
Letting others guide affairs of state
Even though they might be
Lesser men and women.

PROMETHEUS: Such is the doleful hymn of slavery!

IO:

If so, what is this to me?
I have lost my honour and the man I loved.
Rather than live this lingering anguish
It would be better now to end my life.
If I could only find some way to escape.

(ARGUS *applauds silently.* PROMETHEUS *glowers at her.*)

PROMETHEUS:
> If our love meant anything
> It means promise of my freedom, surely,
> And an end to tyranny!

IO:
> **You seem to think our First Minister**
> Will fall from power, Prometheus.

PROMETHEUS: If he does, will you rejoice?

IO:
> I, too, was abused by him
> And denied peace and refuge.

PROMETHEUS: Then it shall happen!

IO:
> Who will remove power from his hands?
> You? Hanging like a moist, torn
> Banner from these rocks?

PROMETHEUS:
> The forces for his overthrow are planted
> And in place. They merely wait
> For the command to strike.

(IO *is confused. Turns to* WORKER, *who stares at* PROMETHEUS.)

IO:
> Will there be more years
> Of hunger and upheaval?
> Armies marching through my father's village—
> Hillsides scorched by fire and neglect?

WORKER: Are you advising us to take up arms against those who've now risen from the revolution? Is this the only road for us?

PROMETHEUS:
> Weapons are the language of the hopeless.
> From time to time the legacy of conflict
> Must be resurrected
> On more than the holidays of state.

WORKER: Arms or no arms? I don't understand.

PROMETHEUS:
> Arms and skillful knowledge of their use
> Are arguments against small-natured

Architects of destiny —
Alert yourselves!
Redefine the tender love
Which knits you to the cosmos
And each other. Pass the banner
Of our struggle to her, she is worthy.
Do so in my name
And I shall be released!

(WORKER *hesitantly reaches into his shirt and takes out a rolled banner which he gives to* IO. *She unfolds it, then bends over it, shuddering.* ARGUS *retreats fearfully from her into shadows, buttoning up his tunic and brushing back his hair as if his personal appearance had to measure up to some standard.*)

IO:

For the infamy and humiliation,
For the scorched harvests
Of my father's fields and life —
For the love of a god-man
Whose words and touch seared
This brain and heart to joy,
All scores shall now be settled!
Weak and frightened though I am
It is better to die
The mother of a hero-people
Than languish in my private pain
And lost illusions
For all that might have been.

(*She exits.* ARGUS *attempts to follow, then exits by a separate route. Drum beats sound, distant and ominous.*)

WORKER: I'm afraid of this wedding of the spirit, Prometheus. Once again I think I hear a trumpet calling for my blood to fuel the engines of history.

FARMER: I'm also afraid.

PROMETHEUS:

More blemished is he
Who betrayed her and now hangs
Suspended from this painful wall —
The gods of the labouring poor
Are as scarred and tarnished, friend
As the street harlot

Or the thief stealing
Medications for his illness —
Like tormentors and murderers
Seeking salvation in the blood of others
Our gods are blemished,
As they grope upwards, eyes averted,
To the frozen slopes
Of their own redemption.

(Drum beats sound louder, nearer.)

PROMETHEUS *(Roaring):*

Think not of yourselves
And your puny dreams of warm hearth
And chirping, milk soured grandchildren
To lighten the heaviness of age!
Think of the burning skull
Nestled on the cruel road to paradise!

(FARMER and WORKER reel under his denunciation.)

PROMETHEUS:

Think of the all-avenging god
His hands and garments bloodied,
His eyes grey and fierce as March gales
On lashing waters of the Atlantic.
Think of bracing gaunt bodies for battle
And the right to rule as you rise,
New men and women,
From the countless dead!
Think of surrender to the whip
And the harsh judgement of the weak
Who make it their affair
To learn the mastery of government!
Prepare yourselves!

FARMER: I'm afraid of something more. Perhaps the judgement of
Prometheus is coloured by the personal harm he has suffered. I
say this with respect, but still I must know, when does personal
tragedy become the concern of everyone?

PROMETHEUS:

No tyrant attacks an entire people.
He selects and isolates his enemies
One by one.

WORKER: You're not afraid of what may happen to you? To all of us?

PROMETHEUS: No.

FARMER: If I must resist, I will. But I'd like more time to weigh what is fact and what is rumour.

PROMETHEUS *(Sarcastically):*
> It is rumoured I am chained
> In an abandoned cavern.

(Sound of drums stops. PROMETHEUS *listens, turns his head and peers into side tunnel.)*

PROMETHEUS:
> I hear footsteps
> Which have walked every hallway
> In the corridors of power.
> It is Hermes, the expediter,
> Himself a holder of no office,
> Yet able to enter unannounced
> The dwellings of generals
> And heads of states.
> A man who, for a fee,
> Will assume any face
> Or point of view.
> Today he must be
> A lackey of our leader
> Who comes to recite some new infamy
> To the detriment
> Of what health I have . . . .

*(*HERMES *enters. Ignores* FARMER *and* WORKER. *Marches directly to* PROMETHEUS.)*

HERMES: Good evening, Prometheus.

PROMETHEUS:
> Good morning, Hermes.
> It is morning.

HERMES *(Checking his watch):*
> It's evening. I watched the sunset
> Before I came here.

PROMETHEUS:
> Counting the seconds
> By my pulse, and adding these
> To make the hours of the day
> I swear it's morning!

(HERMES *checks his watch again, listens to it.* PROMETHEUS *laughs.* HERMES *turns angry.*)

HERMES:
> I'm not here to be made a fool of!
> The crimes you've committed
> Make you no equal of mine!

PROMETHEUS: Can't you see I'm praying?

(HERMES *is flustered and retreats a step.*)

HERMES: I'm sorry. It wasn't my intention to . . . .

PROMETHEUS:
> I'm praying for hangnails, warts
> And slow death by cancer
> For you and your masters!

HERMES: You cannot afford insolence now, Prometheus!

PROMETHEUS:
> I'm happy to be told so . . .
> I felt something had gone wrong.

HERMES:
> Our beloved First Minister's secretary
> Sends a message for you.
> Some provisions can be made
> To facilitate your return to service
> In some minor post yet to be determined.
> Mind you, there will be conditions
> With this offer.

PROMETHEUS: Take your message and insert it . . . .

HERMES *(Angry):* I'm not here to exchange insults with you!

HERMES:
> Your anger comes from stress and paranoia.
> There are drugs for that . . .
> If you should need these, I'd be happy
> To arrange for such.

PROMETHEUS:

>What drugs have you for the hatred
>Which I feel at the sight of you?

HERMES: I don't understand . . . .

PROMETHEUS: Time will teach you all you need to know. Go away!

HERMES:

>You treat me as if my visit here
>Meant nothing . . . as if I were a simple child
>Who wandered in by chance.

(PROMETHEUS *roars with rage.* HERMES *is shaken.*)

PROMETHEUS:

>Do you not understand —
>Do they not know there is no pain
>Or torture which will bow my head
>Before such scum as sent you here
>With options for this village hoodlum?
>They can bomb this place,
>Poison every breath of air I breathe,
>Infect me with disease
>I will not betray the events
>Which will destroy
>This betrayal of our peoples' trust!

HERMES: You had a reputation for some wisdom once.

PROMETHEUS:

>You will not live long enough
>To make an assessment as to who I am!

HERMES *(Pleading):*

>Think for a moment!
>There's no need for stubbornness
>You've lost — accept it
>And take the best deal
>That is offered . . . .

PROMETHEUS:

>You're losing time with me, Hermes.
>Pilferers and thieves
>Are waiting for your service
>In the capital.

(WORKER *and* FARMER *laugh.* HERMES *turns spitefully on them.*)

HERMES:

>This is a private meeting!
>An audience is not permitted!

(FARMER *and* WORKER *stop laughing and face him without moving. He attempts to push them away, but his hands are struck aside. He is pained and shocked.*)

PROMETHEUS:

>This is the outer rim of hell
>On which you stand, Hermes — such displays
>Of petty power are a waste of time.
>I will accept freedom — nothing less.
>Go now — tell them what I said . . . .

HERMES:

>My message . . . has another clause —
>Should you reject the offer I have brought
>Then instructions shall go out
>To attack this cavern with fire and explosives.
>When you are blinded, deafened, your flesh
>Locked in the teeth of crazed rats,
>The airforce will commence an operation
>To reduce everything above and below
>This cavern to smouldering rubble.
>Nothing will be left of you.
>Consider your decision.
>I will wait a moment longer
>And no more.

(*He consults his watch again.* WORKER *and* FARMER *are shaken.*)

WORKER: They plan to attack . . . to bury you! Prometheus . . . spare yourself . . . . A dead martyr is not as useful to us as a living man who can lead us through this time!

(PROMETHEUS *stares at them. Music of* IO'S SONG *is heard playing for one stanza.* PROMETHEUS *tears at his chains and chants.*)

PROMETHEUS:

>He will not destroy me!
>All his weaponry and rockets
>May pulverize the earth —
>May create great firestorms
>Into which entire cities
>Are sucked. An inferno . . .

May boil the oceans
So that mighty tidal waves reach
Beyond the driven clouds
And fall back moaning to a bruised
And aching world . . .
Still, he will not destroy me!
Even though he vaporize my body
And spread its atoms through the cosmos
The will to struggle
For a human order on this earth
Lives on! . . . In the final song
Of victory my name lives on!

HERMES (*Coldly to* WORKER *and* FARMER):
These are delirious cries you hear
Of a once fine mind unhinged,
Driven to betrayal by some disease
Or paranoia of which we have no knowledge—
Dreaming as he does of danger
And persecution
Which never did exist.

WORKER: Who then inflicted this horror that we see?

HERMES: His subversion — and your own.

(WORKER *and* FARMER *stare at* HERMES *with contempt and disbelief.
Another verse of music from* IO'S SONG *is heard.*)

PROMETHEUS:
I dreamed . . . I was hung and left to rot
On a rock in a cold, abandoned cavern . . .
What bastards has our revolution spawned!

(HERMES *motions* WORKER *and* FARMER *to leave.*)

HERMES:
There is nothing you can do to help him.
The manner of his life and death
Are entirely of his choosing.
Let us leave, quickly,
For now the ear-shattering thunder comes
Which will destroy us all
Should we remain.

FARMER: Go by yourself, and tell them who sent you never to sleep
again, for I am unpredictable. I did not leave as they planned I

should . . . I chose to share his suffering, as he suffers for me. Only real traitors are afraid to die before superior arms!

HERMES *(To* WORKER*)*:
> And you? Surely your skills
> And discipline will not allow
> For such ridiculous decisions?

WORKER: I'll stay with him. Tell them whom we elected to kill us, that they've wandered into a desert where a bitter harvest waits for them. Tell them to beware of every living thing which flies, moves or grows from the earth, for it now waits in ambush for them.

PROMETHEUS:
> No! . . . Go with him! You serve nothing
> By remaining here!

WORKER: But Prometheus . . . .

PROMETHEUS:
> In victory or opposition
> I am still your leader!
> I command you to leave
> And take your place
> In the new revolution!

(The attack begins. HERMES *flees. Booming thunder and lightning split the cavern wall to which* PROMETHEUS *is chained. His body is stretched sideways and a wind whips his clothes and hair. One arm chain breaks and* PROMETHEUS, *half-released, hangs shouting at* FARMER *and* WORKER.*)*

PROMETHEUS: Go!

*(*FARMER *and* WORKER *retreat from him and exit. Another attack, and lights flare and die so that* PROMETHEUS *is in silhouette, half kneeling, his arms stretched upwards to remaining wrist shackle. Music of* IO'S SONG *is heard over battle noises, which turn to drum beats as background to his final speech.)*

PROMETHEUS *(Almost fearfully)*:
> They mean to terrify,
> Such is their last bastion
> Of contempt for all that once
> Was decent and time-hallowed . . .

(Another explosion, releasing debris over him)

156

PROMETHEUS:

>. . . They plan once more
To crush this earth,
Burn all the splendid books,
Silence songs of passion and of freedom —
Break the backs of upright men and women,
And look with pride on burning flesh
. . . I am afraid!
And fearful that my mind
May waver, and my voice
Cry surrender . . .
Help me, mother earth!
Help me, winds from the cooling
Restless sea!
Bring water to my lips,
Mother — for the flames
Reaching down towards me
Are more fearful
Than what god might wish us
To endure . . . .

(Another booming blast and flash of light. Scream of PROMETHEUS *over sound. Into sudden darkness and silence.)*

The End

Date Due